THE BEAUTIFUL BRONX

(1920–1950)

THE BEAUTIFUL BRONX

(1920–1950)

Lloyd Ultan

written in collaboration with
The Bronx County Historical Society

ARLINGTON HOUSE·PUBLISHERS
NEW ROCHELLE, NEW YORK

Library of Congress Cataloging in Publication Data

Ultan, Lloyd.
    The beautiful Bronx (1920—1950).

    1. Bronx (Borough)—Social life and customs.
2. New York (City)—Social life and customs. 3. Bronx
(Borough)—Description. 4. New York (City)—Description.
I. Title.
F128.68.B8U57   974.7'275'03   79-15011
ISBN 0-87000-439-5

Manufactured in the United States of America

TO MY PARENTS
who had the wisdom to
raise me in The Bronx

Acknowledgments

A volume such as this cannot see the light of day without a great deal of assistance and encouragement. For their inspiration, guidance, knowledge, and aid, I sincerely thank Michael Miller, Theodore Kazimiroff, Roger Arcara, Nicholas DiBrino, Mr. & Mrs. Walter Fitzgerald, Arthur Seifert, Saul Weber, Sol Elbaum, Bert Gumpert, Ronald Schliessman, Theodore Schliessman, John McNamara, Bert Sack, Raymond Beecher, Pearl London Brooks, Shirley Paris, Brian Danforth, and Florence Palag. For the innumerable services performed, I wish to acknowledge Gary Hermalyn, Laura Tosi, Ann Quinn, Tony King, all from The Bronx County Historical Society, and Kathy Williams, my patient editor, from Arlington House.

Contents

Prologue

"The beautiful Bronx"—that's what we called it. It was an unusual and exciting place to live in those days. In the years from 1920 to 1950, when boom was followed by the Great Depression, which, in turn, was followed by war and another period of prosperity, The Bronx grew from a rural and suburban hinterland of New York City to become a full-fledged part of the thriving metropolis. And we grew up with The Bronx.

In those days following the First World War, millions of people—hard-working, family folk—poured out of the congested tenements of the Lower East Side, East Harlem, and other crowded sections of Manhattan and traveled the rails of the newly built subway lines northward (where most of the lines were elevated) to make a better life for themselves in The Bronx. Why did they come? Because it was "like country." Broad parks, empty lots, tree-lined boulevards, and open farms gave their families the fresh greenery and wholesome air they found desirable in order to raise their children properly.

The newcomers brought with them a variety of backgrounds and customs, which persisted side-by-side with those brought by residents who had settled in The Bronx earlier. It was not uncommon for Irish children to play with Italian children, for Jew to be in the same schoolroom as Gentile, for black to be friends with white. Yet, in the midst of this growing cosmopolitanism, each family lived in a little village called a neighborhood, and each neighborhood usually was dominated by one ethnic group which helped determine the flavor of life for each of the thousands of us growing up in the beautiful Bronx.

Neighborhood Living

We all knew we lived in The Bronx; that was taken for granted. But to those of us growing up in the exciting and turbulent second quarter of the twentieth century, it was the neighborhood that was the center of our lives. It provided us with housing, education, and recreation. And this small area of a few square blocks gave us something tangible, something comprehensible, something very intimate and familiar by which to measure the larger world. Despite the changes going on all around us in those days, the presence of family and friends in the neighborhood made the world seem peaceable, stable, and unchanging.

All the neighborhoods shared many of the same characteristics, but most were unique in their own way, making that neighborhood definable and slightly different from another location perhaps only a few blocks away. Sometimes the difference could be caused by the ethnic group which gave its own cast to a neighborhood; in other cases, it might be caused by the accident of geography, the economic standing of the inhabitants, or the architecture of the buildings.

Mott Haven, for instance, had a large Irish population living in apartment houses built at the turn of the century standing amid still older frame or brick houses, hugging each other as they faced the ever more crowded sidewalks. They were not the only ethnic group in the area; it was a polyglot population. In St. Mary's Park, the children of Jews, Germans, Italians, Greeks, Poles, blacks, and other ethnic groups would mingle their shouts of laughter as they played together and enjoyed each other's company.

A similar scene could be witnessed on the streets of Highbridge. Here the Irish also were the dominant ethnic group, but a walk along Ogden Avenue, the main street of the neighborhood, would reveal sights rarely seen in Ireland. A Lutheran Church near 161st Street on the slope of Ogden Avenue as it descended from the heights of the ridge along which it ran bespoke of the few Scandinavians in the neighborhood. At the other end of the Avenue, near the Washington Bridge, an occasional kosher butcher shop revealed the presence of a Jewish population. But it was such sights as the Noonan Towers apartments and the vast Noonan Plaza apartments and the people dressed in bright green on St. Patrick's Day which told the visitor that the area was largely inhabited by the sons of Erin.

However, it was not the ethnic character of Highbridge which set it off from its neighbors as much as it was the geography. Located on a high bluff at the edge of the Harlem River, which separated The Bronx from Manhattan, most of the east-west streets ended abruptly at the bluff's eastern end. This was a cliff which formed almost a wall ending at Jerome Avenue below. Only at the northern end of Highbridge was this sheer drop ameliorated by the more gentle slope of Boscobel Avenue, which connected the Washington Bridge with 167th Street.

Beyond the Highbridge bluff, extending eastward from Jerome Avenue up to another crest of a hill and sloping down farther eastward from that, was the area called the Grand Concourse. It took its name from the wide boulevard which meandered along the crest of the hill. Here, on either side of the Grand Concourse, the vast majority of the people were Jewish. This was shown by the large number of synagogues which could be seen in the neighborhood. Along 169th Street, west of the great thoroughfare, for instance, there were three in a row. The one on the corner was the elegant Adath Israel, and it was the largest of the three.

However, the Concourse neighborhood was set off not only because of its Jewishness, but also by the economic status of its inhabitants. They were rather well-to-do families, and their status was evident in the uniformed doormen who stood in front of their high class apartment houses. After the Jewish High Holy Day services, men would promenade along the wide tree-lined Grand Concourse wearing their expensive suits, escorting their ladies who were dressed in the latest fashions and furs.

Of course, the Jewish population of Hunts Point, a few miles away, would also attend High Holy Day services dressed in the best they could afford. However, these hard-working people were not as well-to-do as the Jews along the Grand Concourse. Most of them worked hard for a living in a factory, or in a sweatshop as they would call it. Many of them made their living in the needle trades and were strong union men. However, even here, the population was not completely Jewish. There were Irish and Italians in the neighborhood, later to be joined by the Hispanics. Although the Jews were the majority of the population of the area, St. Athanasius Church on Tiffany Street still stood and flourished in the heart of the locality.

Just across the Bronx River from Hunts Point was Clason Point. Although it was simply the other bank of the narrow river, it could have easily been another world. Clason Point was a broad, flat, sandy peninsula that was just about as empty as Hunts Point was crowded. People who lived in the Academy Apartments, or in the brick two-family homes built along the flat streets, shared the neighborhood with the farmers, most of whom were Italian. It was not uncommon to see cows grazing along Soundview Avenue near the point where Commonwealth Avenue crossed it, while people hurried to the trolley which stopped at that intersection to get to work from the attached two-family brick homes along Commonwealth.

A far different sight would greet a visitor to the Belmont area. Hemmed in by Third Avenue, Fordham Road, Southern Boulevard, and Tremont Avenue, this compact neighborhood was almost solidly Italian. Very much like Mott Haven, there were turn-of-the-century apartment houses and older frame houses, although some of the apartments were more modern. However, the flavor of the neighborhood was set by the market strung along Arthur Avenue. Here, produce was not only in the store, but it could be purchased right on the sidewalk. The fresh fruit and vegetables, the salami and sausages, and the pastries gave the street a pungent aroma that made the mouth water. All along

14

the street, shoppers would be haggling with the proprietors of the stands, sometimes speaking in the accents of their native Sicily or Calabria.

A far more calm scene was Riverdale. As with Highbridge, Riverdale was separated from the rest of The Bronx by a high bluff. Unlike Highbridge, many of the Irish who lived there were servants in the large estates which spread across the area. Here, the wealthy lived in their great mansions, and it was common to refer to the Freeman Estate, the Dodge Estate, or the Delafield Estate. Gardeners attended to the mowing of the lawns, the pruning of the century-old trees, the planting of the flowers, and the propagation of new plants. Although the old established families were most prominent, pedigree was not as important as wealth and prominence in enabling one to reside in Riverdale. Anthony Compagna could build his mansion across the street from the huge estate of George Freeman, a partner of J. P. Morgan. Close by, Joseph P. Kennedy resided. It was a comfortable life in a quiet neighborhood.

Far more isolated, however, was City Island. The area was insular in attitude as well as in geography. It was separated from the mainland by a small body of water spanned by a bridge and further separated from its nearest neighbors by the vastness of Pelham Bay Park. Most of the land on the mainland beyond the park consisted of farmland worked by hearty Italians tending their cattle, goats, and potatoes. This made City Island even more distant from the nearest large crowded Bronx neighborhood. On top of that, the whole economy of the island was based on the sea. Shipbuilding, yachting, and seafood dinners were major concerns of those who lived in the frame houses there. This made them different from the rest of The Bronx. They were the clamdiggers, and the others were not, and that was that.

These differences between the Bronxites were real, but, in a larger sense, they were not substantial. In many ways, the people were very much alike. Rich or poor, Catholic, Protestant, or Jew, living on a farm, in a small house, or in an apartment—no matter what the ethnic origin of the family, they were all middle class and embodied middle-class values. The working-class Jews in Hunts Point, for instance, scraping together enough money from their factory work to feed and clothe their families, dreamed of living in the new cream-colored houses with the casement windows and sunken living rooms being built along the Grand Concourse. Like other Bronxites, they wanted to move up in the world, and they worked hard toward that end. If they could not make it for themselves, they would surely make it for their children. And the key to this goal was education.

Every school day in every neighborhood, the spectacle of the children going to school would never vary. The boys, dressed in white shirts with red or blue ties, and the girls, in middy blouses and skirts, would amble along the sidewalk toward the neighborhood school, their schoolbooks in their arms. The schools did not have fancy names. All public schools were known by number. But each one served its surrounding neighborhood, reflecting that neighborhood's population and values. In the vast majority of the cases, the schoolchild absorbed the desire of his parents to get ahead, to improve himself, and to succeed. If anything was wrong at school, the parent would be notified and a conference between the parent and teacher held to straighten out the difficulty. Cooperation between the school and the home was considered to be of prime importance for the advancement of the child.

The school day consisted of a round of instruction in the major subjects of the day. However, the schools were also intent upon molding the young character. Lateness was frowned upon, and all absences had to be fully explained in a doctor's note. The student's dress, considered mandatory, was designed to promote neatness and good grooming. Discipline in the classroom was considered important.

There were times when the tedium of the daily rounds of class instruction was varied by assembly programs, at which all the classes in a single grade marched into the auditorium and took previously assigned seats. Sitting upon chairs on the stage were the principal and other school dignitaries. A color guard made up of four or five classmates had the honor of carrying the flag down the center aisle to the stage. Then all stood, recited the pledge of allegiance, and, led by the music teacher, sang the "Star-Spangled Banner." The principal arose from her seat and read a passage from the Bible, and then introduced the activity of the day. It may have been a speaker who would share his knowledge with the pupils, a film provided by the Bronx Zoo or the Dollar Savings Bank or some other institution, or a play or presentation put on by one of the classes in the school. After that, the assembly would be formally dismissed by the principal, and the students would march back to their classrooms, sit behind desks bolted to the floor, and return to their lessons.

Things were a bit more formal for those whose Catholic parents chose to send them to a parochial school. Often, the boys would be required to wear jackets as well as a tie and white shirt. The girls had to wear a uniform. Some of the parochial schools even required boys to wear a military-style uniform of gray cloth and brass buttons. In these schools, the day was started with prayer, but the instruction in the basic school subjects was just as sound, and the discipline just as prized, as in the public schools.

Once the school day was over, the neighborhood again provided the focus for our lives. After dropping off the schoolbooks at home, and perhaps downing a glass of milk, all the children would dash outside to play with their friends in the neighborhood. Often the meeting place would be a local park. This was natural, since there was hardly a neighborhood which did not have a park close by.

Youngsters in Mott Haven, for instance, would dash to St. Mary's Park to use the playground equipment there. Those in Melrose and the lower part of the Concourse might scramble among the steep rocks of Franz Sigel Park. Crotona Park was the magnet for children in Morrisania and Tremont. The vastness of Van Cortlandt Park occupied the energies of children in Kingsbridge, Riverdale, and Woodlawn.

And if a "gang" of children chose not to go to a park, empty lots were always nearby. They were marvelous places just to wander through. Stones and rocks could always be gathered there, and wildflowers and weeds could be observed. If used long enough, there might be spots in the growth which had grown bare from people running along the prescribed paths of a baseball diamond day after day. If that were the case, it soon became the local baseball field—unofficially, of course. After school, one group of children would take the field and another would challenge the first to a game for the right to use it. The outcome of the game never mattered, since by the time it was completed it was usually time to go home.

The streets also provided us with amusement. In those days, automobile traffic was lighter than it is today and the hazard of being hit by a moving vehicle was not as great. On a quiet sidestreet, a game of stickball might be in progress. Here, the rules were similar to baseball, but the only equipment needed was an old broom handle to serve as a bat and a pink rubber ball manufactured by the Spalding Company, which everyone called a "spaldeen." The playing field was the length of the street. If an old broom handle could not be found, the game was played without it and a clenched fist at the end of the batter's outstretched arm served instead. This variant of the game was called punchball. If there was a broomstick available, but no ball, a round stick tapered at one end would do the trick. Here the tapered stick lying on the ground was struck by the broomstick to flip it in the air. Quickly, the batter then swung his broomstick at the tapered stick while it was in mid-air to hit it as far as he could. This game was called one-a-cat. If there were

16

not that many people available to play a full-fledged game of stickball or punchball, and if a brownstone-like brick building with a long flight of stairs was in the neighborhood, a variant of the game called stoopball was played. Here, the "batter" would hit the spaldeen off the point of the third step in the stone staircase and his companions would try to catch the ball before it bounced. Each time the ball bounced represented a base reached by the imaginary runner. It seems that the variations of the national pastime were endless.

But there were other games played on the streets. There were children who bought bubble gum, and the package always contained cards bearing a color portrait of a baseball player with a short description of his accomplishments printed on the back. Often these cards were traded in an attempt to obtain the full set. Sometimes a game would be devised whereby the cards would be flipped along the sidewalk to the building line. The one whose card landed closest to the building would then keep all the cards flipped in that round. The older boys would do the same, but with pennies.

The regular cracks in the sidewalks were also a means of amusement. Anyone who had a piece of chalk could draw a pattern on the sidewalk. Invariably, the pattern had eight boxes arranged so that the first two numbered boxes shared the same width between cracks, and the third above it had the same width all to itself. The pattern would alternate in this way. Someone would then take a thick piece of wood and throw it on the pattern, trying to hit the first box without touching any crack or chalk borderline. Then he, or she, would step into the pattern, avoiding not only the boundaries of the boxes but also the box in which the wood was resting. The player would hop into each empty box in the pattern and, without leaving it, return to his starting point, stop at the box next to the one with the wood in it, balance himself on one foot, and reach down to pick up the wood before exiting. At this next turn, he would then try to throw the wood into the second numbered box and repeat the process. If the wood fell on a borderline, or if he stepped into the box upon which the wood rested, or if he lost his balance in picking up the wood, he lost his turn. The first person to make it through the complete pattern won the game. We called it potzie.

There were also games played with marbles. Often it was not the formal game where the object was to flip a marble into a drawn circle to hit one already in it. Typically, it was a game played on the street. One person would take a wooden cigar box and cut four or five square holes along the lip of the box in the side where the lid was raised. Removing the lid, he would turn the box upside down in the gutter abutting the curb, so that the side facing the street showed a cigar box with entranceways cut into its side. A player would stoop in the middle of the gutter and shoot his marble (which we always called an immie) toward the box in an attempt to get it into one of the holes. Those that did not get through, the owner of the box kept for himself. If one did thread its way through any of the holes, the player would receive a specified number of immies in addition to his original marble.

Many of these games both boys and girls played together. It was not uncommon to see a girl or two playing stoopball, for instance. However, some games boys would have no part of. Skipping rope was one of these. Two girls held the ends of the rope and turned it while a third skipped over it reciting a rhythmic chant, which always began, "A, my name is Alice. . . ." If she completed the entire chant without tripping on the rope, she would then go to the next chant, in which most of the words started with the letter "B." This would continue, in theory, until the entire alphabetical system of chants was completed. However, invariably, the skipper would trip up somewhere, and then one of the holders would skip while the former skipper would take her place holding one end of the rope. The game was so long and drawn out that few ever completed the alphabet.

The girls also played other games. Jacks was popular, whereby the girl would bounce a spaldeen, pick up one of the intricately crossed pieces of metal called a "jack" before the ball could bounce again, and catch the ball in mid-air in the same hand that held the jack. If she missed, she would lose her turn and her companion would try. This would continue until all the jacks were picked up and the girl having the most won the game.

Girls, of course, had their dolls, and often they would try to coax boys into playing house with them. This most boys were reluctant to do, but they would participate on occasion.

For the youngster growing up then, his dwelling, his school, and his playmates formed the nucleus of his world. Warm, comfortable, and seemingly unchanging as it was, he could venture beyond it.

Getting Around

For children growing up in The Bronx between 1920 and 1950, traveling was fairly easy. Public transportation was readily available, cheap, and easy to use. Moreover, it was a conduit which took us out of our neighborhoods into the wider world of The Bronx and its surroundings.

Perhaps the most familiar way to get around was by trolley car. Riding one of these red and yellow wooden cars was very much of an adventure. The tracks were embedded in the street and held in place by brick-shaped stones called Belgian block, but which we always called cobblestones. Overhead, supported by poles erected on the sidewalk, were the wires which provided the electric power for the trolley car. Customers would wait on the sidewalk until one of the cars came along, its steel wheels grinding against the steel rails. As it approached the stop, the people would venture out into the street to the tracks to board the trolley. The accordion doors would open, the wooden steps would be revealed, and each passenger would then ascend them, placing a nickel in the fare box. As each coin was deposited, a loud clanging bell was triggered to register the fare. The passengers would then seat themselves in the wicker seats, each one seating two people and all facing in the same direction.

There were special pleasures in riding the trolley cars. In the summertime, the wooden frames holding the windows at the side of the car would be removed. They would be replaced with chicken-wire fences made of iron which reached to the shoulder of the seated passenger. Thus, with the side of the car now open to the air, the cooling breeze created as the trolley car glided through the streets of The Bronx would waft over the passengers, affording them welcome relief from the heat.

Whenever the trolley reached a point where two lines using the same track diverged into different directions, the motorman stopped his car, opened the door, took an iron poker which had rested upright in a slot near him, alighted from the car, and used the poker to align the tracks at the junction so that the car would proceed to its proper destination. Such sights were frequent at the eastern end of the Washington Bridge near

University Avenue, where the University Avenue, Ogden Avenue, 183rd Street Crosstown, and 167th Street Crosstown trolleys coming from 181st Street in Manhattan diverged. The cars that shared the tracks at West Farms Square also had to have that operation performed.

Of course, riding a trolley to the end of the line would produce another treat. The loop at the end of Soundview Avenue which enabled trolley cars on that line to simply circle around to head in the opposite direction was rare. Normally, the car came to its final stop, and the pole arising from the rear of the car connecting it to the power source of the overhead wire was hauled down by a rope attached at its end. After the pole had been made to lie parallel to the top of the car, the rope was securely tied to prevent it from rising of its own volition. Then the pole in the front of the car, which had been tied in the same position, was released, and the spring at its base would cause it to fly up to the overhead wire, tamed only by the man guiding it with the attached rope. Then the seats inside the car would be similarly transformed. The iron frame holding the wicker back of a seat could, in one motion, be moved to what had been the front end of the seat. By this maneuver, in practically no time at all, the seats which had been facing one direction were now facing the other. The motorman, who had removed his equipment for operating the trolley car from what had been the front end, now reattached it to the similar equipment at the other end. To children's eyes, it seemed that miraculously the trolley car had turned around without changing its position.

Sometimes, some of the older, bolder boys would try to ride the trolley cars for free. We would call it hitching a ride. Rather than enter the car and pay a fare, a boy would try to find a toehold and a place to grasp his hands on the rear. It would be exciting holding on for dear life as the scenery passed by at what seemed to be unbelievable speed. Of course, it was dangerous, and that added to the thrill. Luckily, in those days, automobile traffic was much lighter. At times, one of the bold boys would pull a prank by tugging at the wire connected to the pole transferring the electric power from the overhead wire to the trolley car. With the power cut off, the car would coast, slowing down to a halt. Nothing aroused the ire of the motorman more, and the only recourse for the errant boy was to run as fast as his legs would carry him, laughing at the sputtering anger of a frustrated motorman who could never hope to catch him.

But no one had to hitch a ride on a trolley to enjoy the scenery. The ride was slow enough to absorb the passing views, yet fast enough to register the sweep of change as the panorama of the various Bronx neighborhoods unfolded outside the car window. Moreover, it was smooth. No bumps in the roadway were there to jar the nerves, since the steel tracks made everything level. In fact, the only discomfort, if it could be called a discomfort, was the attempts by the trolley cars to ascend some of the steeper hills. Kingsbridge Road from Bailey Avenue to Sedgwick Avenue was notorious. The hill at 163rd Street east of Third Avenue seemed to push the seated passengers back on their spines. But, in a sense, this was part of the fun, and seeing the changing scenery added to it.

Boarding the 138th Street Crosstown trolley at the East River, there was a scene of bustling activity. Amid the factories and warehouses in the neighborhood, there loomed a complex of old red-brick buildings which stretched over several blocks along 138th Street and dominated it. This was the plant of R. Hoe and Company, the manufacturers of printing presses and saws, as the metal sign flanking the main entrance stated proudly. Every day at the evening rush hour the cars would fill with the plant workers on their way home. As the trolley car passed Eastern Boulevard, the scene became at once more residential and more commercial. Five-story brick apartment houses standing side by side, their cornices almost forming a single uninterrupted line from block to block, rose on each side of the street. However, on the sidewalk level in each building were shops attracting the housewives of the neighborhood. Grocery stores, dress shops, furniture shops, dry cleaners, and more were available for the convenience of any resident. At Alexander Avenue rose St. Jerome's Church, with its onion shaped cupola covering its bell tower at the corner of 138th Street. As the trolley ambled along to Third Avenue, where Lincoln Avenue intersected the junction with 138th Street to form triangles north and south of the trolley route, the memorial to the neighborhood dead of the First World War could be seen. A bald eagle with wings outstretched stood atop a Grecian column, at the base of which were inscribed the names of the fallen. Beyond that, the scene quickly changed to industrial once again. Here could be found coal yards and piano factories, but the Victorian red-brick New York Central Mott Haven railroad station dominated the landscape.

Farther north, the Tremont Avenue trolley afforded its passengers a wider variety of views. Beginning its run on Burnside Avenue in the University Heights area, not too far from the New York University campus, the trolley would descend the steep hill to the Jerome Avenue elevated subway station below, where passengers could transfer to the Lexington Avenue line, or to the Sixth and Ninth Avenue Els. The car would proceed up the hill, flanked by apartment houses, to the underpass that whisked the passengers under the Grand Concourse until the trolley finally made its rendezvous with Tremont Avenue at Webster Avenue. Here, the Webster Avenue, the 183rd Street Crosstown, and the Tremont Avenue trolleys met. The car would continue on its way along Tremont Avenue, flanked by a variety of shops attracting more than just the people from the immediate neighborhood. On past the headquarters of the Bronx Savings Bank and over the railroad tracks at Park Avenue (with the Western Union station conveniently located inside the Tremont Station of the New York Central), the trolley wended its way, passing the bustling commercial area until it arrived at Third Avenue. Here, passengers could catch the Third Avenue El or get off to climb the steep flight of stairs leading to the yellow and brown Bronx Borough Hall atop a high bluff at the corner. The trolley would continue up a gentle rise, past the Bergen Building, the neighborhood shops and apartment houses, and the elegant old apartments on Southern Boulevard, down a steep hill under the very high elevated subway structure on Boston Road into West Farms Square. Here was the meeting place of several trolley lines, and passengers would get off and on, transferring from one to another. Others would take the nearby subway. A main attraction at this stop was the Starlight Amusement Park and the Colosseum. However, its journey not yet completed, the Tremont Avenue trolley would continue on its way, passing these attractions, to the relatively flat surface of the eastern part of The Bronx. Beyond West Farms Square, it would thread its way between the New Haven Railroad tracks on one side and the spacious wooded grounds of the Catholic Protectory on the other. It would pass by St. Raymond's Church at Castle Hill Avenue, and then follow the curves of Tremont Avenue into Westchester Square. Here was another commercial center for a neighborhood, with shops flanking the wide square. In the center was a park where people could rest after dashing from one store to another. Looming overhead along Westchester Avenue was the elevated station of the Pelham Bay local of the Lexington Avenue subway. The trolley, however, still went on its way, past the lumber yard and over the bridge crossing Westchester Creek. Here, the pace of life seemed much slower. The shops flanking the street were now in taxpayers (one- or two-story structures containing only shops) and apartment houses were rare. In fact, any look out of the trolley window would reveal single family frame houses. Once past the open spaces of St. Raymond's Cemetery, the trolley car finally reached the end of the line at Eastern Boulevard. On this one journey, any traveler could see the entire panorama of Bronx life, from apartment houses, to stores, to a government center, to parks, to frame houses—all for only a nickel.

Boarding the Fordham Road trolley would bring different views of The Bronx. After coming over the 207th Street Bridge from Manhattan, the trolley would strain mightily up the steep hill to Sedgwick Avenue. Apartment houses on the south side of the street had shops in their sidewalk level even this far west. On the north end of the street, the great gas tank dominated the scene, and then the Webb Shipbuilding Academy, an ornate Victorian pile. At Jerome Avenue, with its elevated subway almost acting as if it were a gateway arch, the main shopping center started. In addition, this was also the center for theaters. Near Jerome Avenue, there was the Loew's Grand. Beyond Jerome Avenue, amid all the shops and department stores, there were others. The Concourse, the RKO Fordham, the Valentine, and the Windsor all could be seen from the trolley window. Beyond the Grand Concourse, the car descended the hill past Roger's Department Store and stopped at Third Avenue. Here, the Fordham Road station of the famous elevated line seemed to form an arch which signaled the end of the shopping center. A small park occupied the corner to the north, next to the Fordham station of the New York Central. Beyond the elevated structure, the shops petered out. Fordham University, with its Gothic buildings, could be seen to the north as the trolley continued its journey. Across the street, Theodore Roosevelt High School occupied a cream-colored building with a classical portico. The journey ended at Southern Boulevard. Here, a passenger could visit an ailing relative at Fordham Hospital, but, more likely, most passengers were on their way to the Bronx Zoo or the Botanical Garden.

There were other lines, of course, and each had its share of adventure and surprise. It was very easy to ride on all of them since the nickel fare would also entitle any passenger to a transfer. With this slip of paper, the trolley rider could get off a Crosstown car and board an intersecting north-south trolley at no additional cost.

While trolleys were numerous, unfortunately, they did not go everywhere. There were buses which plied other routes. For some unknown reason, 170th Street was serviced by a bus, not a trolley. The exclusive Grand Concourse had two buses, one going down to 138th Street and the other leaving the Concourse at 165th Street to go to the Hub at 150th Street and Melrose Avenue. Another bus paralleled the trolley from Sedgwick Avenue along Fordham Road, but continued on to Pelham Parkway and City Island. While the buses could run faster than the trolley cars, somehow they were not as much fun to ride. The chugging engine and the vagaries of roadway repair usually made the ride bumpy. The windows of a bus seemed more narrow than a trolley's, too. Certainly, the sides could not come out of a bus in the summertime, and a ride on one at that time could be stifling.

But riding subways and elevated lines was much more fun. On the els, not only was the train going faster than a trolley car, but it was going just as smoothly over steel rails too. In addition, there was the added advantage of being situated high over the street, and a panoramic view could be seen out the windows. Moreover, since most of the subway lines in The Bronx were also elevated, the same situation could be applied to them.

The shortest of these rides in The Bronx was along the Broadway line. Boarding the train at 242nd Street and Broadway, the view not only encompassed the expanse of the southern end of Van Cortlandt Park but, as the train proceeded, the entire panorama of Kingsbridge and Riverdale was revealed. The high bluff that separated Riverdale from the rest of The Bronx could be easily seen, with some houses, and even a rare apartment house, clinging to the edge. In the other direction, the hill leading up to Kingsbridge Heights was dotted with the fine homes and occasional small apartment houses that dotted the hillside. However, the most spectacular sight of The Bronx on the Broadway line could be seen only after the train had crossed Spuyten Duyvil Creek into Manhattan. As the train passed above Manhattan streets, there was a spectacular view of the New York University campus and the Hall of Fame across the Harlem River.

Farther east was the Jerome Avenue line. Leaving the Woodlawn station, part of the broad expanse of Woodlawn Cemetery could be seen out of one window, while one of the golf courses in Van Cortlandt Park could be viewed out of the other. As the train continued down the line, the square tower of DeWitt Clinton High School rose in the distance over Mosholu Parkway. Beyond that, the new Gothic buildings of the Hunter College campus could be seen at Bedford Park Boulevard, with the wide Jerome Park Reservoir behind it. At Kingsbridge Road, a passenger could almost touch the wall of the vast Kingsbridge Armory which seemed to abut the station. Then onward, passing St. James' Park and picturesque St. James' Church, to Fordham Road and the beginning of the shopping district there. Below Fordham Road, the rear of the apartments which faced parallel streets could be seen. The windows that faced the setting sun had their awnings drawn in the summertime to keep out the heat. The clatter of the train echoed against the buildings' sides and returned with a roar as the train sped down the Jerome Avenue corridor. Below 167th Street, the view widened out again over Mullaly Park to the escarpment that separated Highbridge from the rest of The Bronx. At 161st Street, Yankee Stadium came into view and a quick glance after leaving the station would give the passengers a view of the field over the bleacher wall. Many would strain to see part of the action of a game in progress. However, the train would soon plunge into the darkness of a subway tunnel and all such views would end.

For a great part of the line, the Sixth and Ninth Avenue Els shared the same tracks. Below 167th Street, the el trains would go onto their own line and dip below the Jerome Avenue tracks until they made a sharp turn just north of the sidewalk at 162nd Street. Here was a spectacular view of Yankee Stadium, only one block away, and the broad expanse of Mullaly and Macombs Dam Parks. Oddly, the el trains entered a tunnel at the Jerome-Anderson Avenues station, traveling under the Highbridge neighborhood and emerging at the other end at Sedgwick Avenue before crossing into Manhattan for a stop at the Polo Grounds. For those living in Highbridge, the anomaly was all too evident. While there were many places in the city where people had to go up to an elevated station to take the subway, Anderson Avenue, as far as anyone knew, was the only place where a passenger had to go downstairs into the ground to get an elevated train. Moreover, this peculiarity continued, for when the elevated line was abandoned in Manhattan, it continued to be used in The Bronx as a shuttle between 167th Street and the Polo Grounds.

Farther east was the Third Avenue El. Unless it were rush hour (when the train would start at 241st Street), the journey would begin at Gun Hill Road, where the el station was lodged beneath the elevated subway station one level above. Pulling out, the train would pass over the Bronx River Parkway and give the passengers a beautiful view of the Bronx River valley. Turning onto Webster Avenue, the train would pass near the upper reaches of Bronx Park and parts of the Botanical Garden could be glimpsed through the window. Just before entering the Fordham Road station, the Gothic towers of Fordham University could be seen. Below that station, the train traveled over Third Avenue, and the buildings seemed to crowd toward the el structure as it proceeded on its course. At Tremont Avenue, the Bronx Borough Hall was easily seen outside the window. Standing there on its high hill, it reached the same level as the el train. Many often wondered why no causeway from the train station directly to the building was ever constructed, since that would save passengers the trouble of walking down the stairs of the el and up the stairs to the building. South of Tremont Avenue, many older apartment houses faced the el structure, and passing passengers could easily see people inside leaning out of their windows as the train rumbled by. At 161st Street, the train, following the course of Third Avenue, turned a corner around the old courthouse there and in a niche, facing the train windows, was a seated statue of justice over the courthouse entrance. As the train sped toward the commercial center of the Hub, the tops of department stores and advertising signs could be seen trying to influence the passengers. Perhaps the weirdest part of the journey started at 144th Street. There, the train veered off Third Avenue onto its own right of way between Alexander and Willis Avenues. It was as if the train were passing through the backyard between two sets of apartment houses. All the qualities of backyard life in The Bronx could be seen, down to the ubiquitous wash hanging out to dry for the inspection of the el passengers.

Of course, there were other branches of the Third Avenue El in The Bronx. One branch began at a spur near the Botanical Garden and quickly joined the main line at Fordham Road. Another traveled over the subway tracks from the Freeman Street station down Southern Boulevard and Westchester Avenue until it left them to go down Bergen Avenue to connect with the main line at 143rd Street.

The subway tracks that this branch of the Third Avenue El followed were on the White Plains Road line, which began at 241st Street. There, along the upper reaches of that line, was a spectacular view of the countryside. There were a few apartment houses nearby that blocked the view, but, in general, frame houses and taxpayers dominated the Wakefield and Williamsbridge areas. An exception was the huge Victorian Gothic Crawford Memorial Church at 218th Street. Looking east, a passenger could see some of the farms under cultivation. Looking west, there was a panoramic view of Woodlawn Cemetery across the Bronx River Valley. Apartments came into view in the vicinity of Burke Avenue, but there were fine views of Bronx Park below Pelham Parkway. After the 180th Street station, the train crossed the Bronx River valley and the factories and coal yards in that neighborhood could be easily seen. Below West Farms Square, the apartment houses again closed in to block the view until, just before plunging underground at Third Avenue, the wholesale meat markets along Westchester Avenue could be glimpsed.

The easternmost line was the Pelham Bay local. Like the upper reaches of the White Plains Road line, the train, proceeding out of the Pelham Bay Park station, would pass by taxpayers and single family homes, affording the passenger a wide view of the flat, green countryside. It was a pleasant ride, passing by Westchester Creek at Westchester Square and the Catholic Protectory at 177th Street. While some apartments began to impinge on the view in the Soundview section, a look down the streets between them revealed the farms and empty lots beyond. Soon after crossing the Bronx River, passing by the Metropolitan Pool at Whitlock Avenue, this line, too, took the plunge into the stark blackness of a subway tunnel.

Of course, things did change. There was a railroad line called the New York, Westchester, and Boston, which everyone called the Westchester, that had operated electrically powered railroad cars for commuters. It was fast, but it stopped at the New Haven Railroad yards near the Willis Avenue Bridge. Passengers had to transfer there, for an extra fare, to a spur of the Third Avenue El and then transfer again to the main line at 125th Street in Manhattan. With this inconvenience, it is no wonder that the line went bankrupt during the Depression. However, the tracks north of 180th Street were bought by the city and were made a part of the subway system as the Dyre Avenue line. When reopened, it was a shuttle only, traveling back and forth between Dyre Avenue and 180th Street, where passengers could transfer to the White Plains Road line. The view was almost non-existent, for most of this line ran in a trench and nothing really could be seen except the back of the old Westchester's ornate headquarters building at 180th Street, which was now used by the subway.

Another addition was the Concourse IND Sixth and Eighth Avenue Subway, built to replace the destroyed Sixth and Ninth Avenue Els. Here, for the first time, an entire

24

subway line ran underground in The Bronx, and there was no opportunity to see any sights along its route.

However, that did not mean that a child could not have fun underground in a subway train. The secret was to enter at the first car and peer through the large glass window at the front. Ahead was a perfect view of the tunnel, the tracks illuminated by the lights gleaming from the first car of the train. At intervals there were incandescent light bulbs by which the dimensions of the tunnel could be discerned and flashing red and green lights informing the motorman whether to proceed or to halt. The rush of the train through the darkness, pierced by intervals of light, seemed much faster than it actually was because the tunnel walls were so close to the train and the rumble was magnified by them. It was fun to imagine being the motorman, seated behind his cubicle nearby, trying to run the train.

Even if a child were not seated in the first car, there were other ways to find amusement underground. In the IRT cars, the seats were arranged with their backs to the windows and the passengers had to face each other. Who were those people on the other side of the aisle? What did they do for a living? Where would they get off? It was a good guessing game.

In the summertime, the wide four-bladed exposed fans overhead in each car were activated, moving the air around in the enclosed space. Sometimes it was amusing just to watch someone standing under the whirring fan trying to keep his hair in place while the fan constantly mussed it.

There was also amusement in watching the conductor on the subway trains. His responsibility was to open and close the doors, and the mechanism for doing so was located between two cars in the center of the train. At each station, up he would get on his perch, pressing the buttons to open the doors, looking intently down either end of the platform to be sure that each waiting passenger was well inside before closing them again, muttering under his breath as latecomers made a mad dash for the doors before they closed. These latecomers had a better chance with the IRT cars than with the newer IND ones. The IRT had large single doors, three to each side of a car. If a door were closing, a latecomer could usually find an opening still wide enough to pass through until it finally locked in place. This was not so with the IND. There, each opening had double doors, both closing in tandem, meeting at midpoint in the aperture. Because of this, the IND doors closed twice as fast as the IRT, and an opening quickly vanished. But it was fun to watch the game between conductor and latecomer.

Nevertheless, the trolleys, the buses, and the subways were not there just for fun. They could and did whisk people from one place to another quickly and efficiently for a reasonable price.

Places to Go

Although Manhattan was known worldwide for its many sights, The Bronx had its share of places to go. They were located in all areas of the borough, and public transportation made them accessible to anyone old enough to put a nickel in a fare box.

The Bronx Zoo, of course, was a major attraction. It never ceased to fascinate any child. Grouped around the seal pool in the northern section of the zoo, not too far from Fordham Road, were several orange-brick houses drawing groups of people to their outside cages. The Lion House, with its majestic carved lions guarding the entrance, featured not only the king of beasts, but also tigers, panthers, leopards, and other big jungle cats. Across the way at the Monkey House, the antics of the creatures swinging from one section of the cage to the other were fun to watch. The white, domed Elephant House housed not only the great pachyderms, but also the rhinoceros and the hippopotamus. In front of the Elephant House was a ring where a child could beg his parents to buy him a ride on a camel. Nearby was the Children's Zoo, a very special area, where the entry rules were reversed. Here, a child was charged a higher admission fee than his parent, and no adult was permitted to enter unless accompanied by a child. Inside, the children could touch, pet, and feed some of the smaller and tamer farm animals kept there. There was also the Farm in the Zoo, serving to introduce city children to live farm animals, such as cows and pigs. The bear den was a delight as the polar bears splashed around in their pool and the brown bears climbed the steep crag in which their cave was located.

But the animals were not the only attraction in the Bronx Zoo. North of the West Farms gate was the Rocking Stone, a large boulder resting on a point. When pushed, it would gently rock back and forth. Nearby, the Rocking Stone Restaurant was a convenient resting place for a meal. Snacks were available at several points in the park, and there were places where special animal food could be purchased for anyone who wanted the thrill of feeding a wild beast. Naturally, this produced trash, and scattered throughout the ground were receptacles disguised as tree stumps. In them, Cracker Jack boxes and cellophane wrappers could be discarded. After the World's Fair of 1939–40, the Zoo acquired the Fair's tractor-train. With this, people who entered the Zoo at the West Farms gate at the southern end could be quickly transported through the grounds to the Lion House and other attractions close to the Concourse entrance near Fordham Road. Similarly, those at the northern end of the Zoo could board the tractor-train there to return. It was very popular and certainly saved a lot of walking. However, those strolling through the grounds had to quickly step aside as it whisked by.

The best time to be at the Bronx Zoo was at feeding time. At the Lion House, just before the keeper arrived, the big cats would growl. Increasingly, more cats would add their voices until it reached a crescendo of roaring, which seemed to hail the entrance of the keeper. As a large chunk of meat was pushed into each cage, the occupant would pounce on it, greedily gnawing at it. At the seal pool, feeding time was less menacing and more amusing. At the appointed hour, the keeper arrived with a bucket of fish. Almost all the sea-lions in the enclosure would jump off the artificial rock upon which they sunned themselves and splash into the pool, huddling near the keeper with his precious load of fish. Reaching his hand into his bucket, the keeper would toss a fish to one side of the pool and a second toward the other side, always making sure that all the pool's residents would receive a fair share of the goodies. Often the sea-lions would jump up to meet the fish in mid-air, provoking cries of glee from the children watching.

Across Fordham Road from the Bronx Zoo was the Botanical Garden. Here, the main attraction was the great greenhouse complex called the Conservatory. Inside, exotic plants from tropical climates were growing. In one section, the lush green foliage of the jungle arched over the walkways inside, and the climate was deliberately kept very hot and humid so that the plants would thrive. One step inside this section, sweat would pour and the clothes would begin to cling to the body. Another section featured varieties of cactus and other desert plants. Here the climate was just as hot, but it was more bearable because it was kept dry. In the center of the Conservatory, under its great glass cupola, were the palm trees, some so tall that they seemed to be scraping the high roof.

The best time to visit the Botanical Garden was in the springtime, when all the colorful spring flowers bloomed and filled the meadows there with their fragrant scents. Whether one looked at daffodils or rose bushes, spring in the Botanical Garden was a spectacular sight.

However, there was more to the Botanical Garden than flowers in the meadow and exotic plants in the Conservatory. It was a beautiful place no matter what time of year. There were meadows where no buildings outside the Garden could be seen. Only the lovely hills and rock outcroppings surrounded the viewer, and at that point it was hard to realize that this beautiful spot was in the middle of a city. A walk through the Hemlock Grove, the only virgin forest left, was a delight, and a view of the gorge of the Bronx River with its picturesque waterfall was spectacular. Nearby was the stone Lorillard Snuff Mill, then used as a storage area. Beyond that was the wooden Lorillard Mansion which, until it burned down in the mid-1920s, served as a small museum of art and science.

There were other historic houses in The Bronx to visit after the Lorillard Mansion burned down. In Van Cortlandt Park, there was the Van Cortlandt Mansion. This old stone house was filled with fine colonial furniture, and the caretaker would tell you, if asked, that George Washington had visited the place several times. One room featuring a fireplace decorated with blue and white delft Dutch tiles had cases with exhibits.

Attracting more people was Poe Cottage in Poe Park at Kingsbridge Road and the Grand Concourse. In this neat wooden house, Edgar Allan Poe had lived, and the old caretaker there would take pride in pointing to the bed in which Poe's wife had died and to the rocking chair that the famed poet had used. The house seemed pitifully small for such a great writer, but it was a shrine to which Poe devotees had to make a pilgrimage at least once.

Not too far from Poe Cottage stood the Hall of Fame for Great Americans on the New York University campus. This colonnade, perched at the edge of a high hill overlooking the Harlem River Valley, had been established to honor those Americans who had made significant contributions to the country and to mankind. Busts of those elected were to stand in the niches between the columns. However, to a child, the Hall of Fame was disappointing. Then there were fewer niches filled than today, and there was not as much to see. The only worthwhile thing about the visit seemed to be the magnificent view of the river valley and of the hills of northern Manhattan across the way. We were assured by our teachers in school that the number of people elected to the Hall of Fame every five years would increase the number of busts on display and that each time we would visit there would be more to see. They were right.

If there was one major attraction for which The Bronx was noted throughout the country, it was Yankee Stadium. Built in 1922–23, and opening in April 18, 1923, with Governor Alfred E. Smith throwing out the first ball, it became the Home of Champions. While Jacob Ruppert provided the money and Miller Huggins provided the managerial talent, the man who drew the crowds was Babe Ruth. For a ballplayer, Ruth was ridiculously built, with his heavy torso balanced on spindly legs. But anyone who saw him play could never argue against his talent. Not only could he clout home runs into the right field stands, but he could play defense at his position in right field as few have ever done. It was not without reason that the Stadium was called "The House That Ruth Built."

Babe Ruth had no peer, but he was not the only talent on the New York Yankees. He was joined by first baseman Lou Gehrig, who could hit line drive home runs into the lower stands with amazing regularity. Although not as flashy as Ruth, he was steady and reliable. He was always there, and for many years he never missed a game until he contracted a tragic disease that forced his retirement.

By that time, a new star was rising in the Yankee ball club—Joe DiMaggio. Because he was right-handed, the balls he hit were batted toward left field, where the fences were not as close as right field, where Ruth and Gehrig had aimed their cannons. Many of DiMaggio's hits might have been home runs if he had had an equal chance. However, he was also a home-run king and a consistent hitter. Moreover, his defensive play in center field was marked with grace and ease.

Ruth, Gehrig, and DiMaggio were the trinity of the New York Yankee fans, but they were not the only outstanding players. With rare exception, the team was strong at every position, and it regularly had the best pitching staff in the game. Year after year the Yankees won American League pennants, usually winning the World Series afterward. So powerful were the Yankees that the team under Miller Huggins in the 1920s was nicknamed "Murderers' Row," and the Yankees of the 1930s under manager Joe McCarthy were called "The Bronx Bombers." After a while, it was taken for granted that the Yankees would win. It seemed natural.

On the day of a game, thousands of people would stream to Yankee Stadium by subway and trolley car, cramming the streets and overflowing the sidewalks into the gutter. Police had to be especially assigned for traffic duty to handle the crowds. It was exciting just to be in the crowd, being jostled on the streets, confronted by the people selling souvenirs along the pathways to the stadium, and swept up the ramps inside the big ball park to the seats. There, under the large roof bearing the distinctive scallop design, spectacular plays in the field would be cheered loudly, with the thousands of voices echoed and re-echoed as the cheers bounced off the cavernous walls.

However, Yankee Stadium was not known simply for baseball. Other sports events happened there too. There were times when college football was an attraction, especially the "Battle of The Bronx" between New York University and Fordham. Professional football was tried in the 1940s, when the New York Football Yankees of the All-America Conference used the Stadium as its home. The Stadium was also the scene for some championship boxing matches. Perhaps the most unforgettable one was the Joe Louis-Max Schmeling bout on June 22, 1938, when Louis pounced upon the German, raining blows upon him and knocking him out in the first round. But baseball was the national pastime, and it was baseball for which Yankee Stadium had been built and which gave it its fame.

These were the things that the out-of-towners who visited New York City came up to The Bronx to see. Like us, they might stroll through the Bronx Zoo, amble about the Botanical Garden, visit the Van Cortlandt Mansion, be attracted to Poe Cottage, examine the busts at the Hall of Fame, and cheer the home runs at Yankee Stadium. But they did not know The Bronx as we did.

IV

Diversions

There were a variety of opportunities for people of all ages to be entertained in the beautiful Bronx. Probably foremost was the public library. There was always time for reading, and a library card was the key that opened up whole worlds of experiences buried in the printed word. Once received, it was used again and again. All anyone had to do was to choose the books he wished to borrow and present his card to the librarian at the desk. She would use a dating stamp affixed to the back of a pencil to mark the date when the book should be returned, both on the book's card (which she kept) and on a form pasted inside the cover (for the borrower's information).

For two weeks, a borrower could explore the works of Richard Halliburton describing the exotic corners of the world with romantic words, or suffer with Scarlett O'Hara in Margaret Mitchell's best seller **Gone with the Wind,** or agonize over the predicaments in which Nancy Drew or the Hardy Boys managed to find themselves. After absorbing whatever the books had to reveal, the borrower returned them, and a new set was borrowed to take the reader along new flights of fancy.

In general, the libraries themselves were impressive places. The one on Alexander Avenue and the one on 169th Street near McKinley Square, for instance, looked very much like private mansions. The Melrose branch on Morris Avenue and 162nd Street was three stories high, and the children's room was on the third story, to be reached only by an arduous climb up a staircase that was relatively steep for small legs. The Highbridge branch atop the Shakespeare Avenue hill on 168th Street was smaller, but its white facade with brick trim and high arched windows made it an impressive and cheery place. This was a far cry from the Kingsbridge branch, which was located on the second floor of a two-story taxpayer.

Perhaps the most unusual library in The Bronx was located on the south side of Westchester Square. There stood the small Huntington Free Library. Entering through a square tower which proclaimed its beginning in 1890, the reader was ushered into a wood-paneled room lined with books. The ceiling rose to the high point of the roof, supported by wooden struts carved in the Victorian Gothic manner. The librarian was always helpful in finding whatever the readers needed, but this collection was not part of the public library system and the books could not be taken home. They had to be read there.

However, if you got your books from the public library, as most people did, where would you read them? A perfect choice on a fine summer day would be the local park. Sitting on a bench, in the shade of a tree, it would be easy to forget the loveliest of surroundings if the book were absorbing. Even the smallest parks could be attractive in those circumstances. The strip along University Avenue, equipped with benches, was perfect for reading, as was the tiny Melrose Park at 161st Street and Park Avenue. Another strip of park in the middle of Mount Eden Avenue on either side of the Concourse was also a good location for sitting on a bench and reading, as were the little triangles at Fordham Road and Creston Avenue and in McKinley Square. The larger park in the middle of Westchester Square could also be used for reading.

But a park was good for things other than reading. If it had playground equipment, as St. Mary's Park, Mullaly Park, Williamsbridge Oval Park, and others did, it was easy to find diversion on the swings, see-saws, slide upons, and monkey bars. If it was large, such as Van Cortlandt Park or Pelham Bay Park, there were other wonders to behold. In the marshlands could be seen wildlife without the interference of bars or cages as in the Bronx Zoo. Turtles, rabbits, raccoons, egrets, and other beasts not found on the streets of The Bronx could be spotted there. In addition, both of those parks were equipped with riding academies, and it was possible to learn to ride the horses and take them along the bridle path in Van Cortlandt Park or along Pelham Parkway.

It was also possible to go boating in the parks. At Indian Lake in Crotona Park, boats could be rented. It was pleasant to row along the placid water, passing by the old folks seated at the northern end of the lake playing chess. Another boathouse was located by the lake in Van Cortlandt Park. Perhaps the most popular boating facility was the boathouse in Bronx Park along the banks of the Bronx River, across from the West Farms entrance to the Bronx Zoo.

But boating was not confined to the parks. At the marina on the Highbridge shore just north of Yankee Stadium, boats were berthed which could ply the Harlem River. Along the shores of Long Island Sound and the East River, in Clason Point, Ferry Point, Castle Hill, Throgs Neck, and Baychester, other boats were kept for use there. However, the chief center for sailing in The Bronx was City Island. Here boats were not only berthed, but constructed as well, and it was a rare summer's Sunday when one did not see the island encircled with sails tacked to the breeze.

On a hot summer day, water was also for swimming. It was fun to sneak down to the less frequented spots along the Harlem or Bronx Rivers and dip into the water, without benefit of a bathing suit, to cool off. Of course, there were several places where swimming was encouraged. The bungalow colonies of Harding Park, Silver Beach, and Edgewater Park, all near the eastern seashore, were some of them. In Pelham Bay Park in the 1920s, another one grew. There, the rockbound coast of the park was dotted with temporary wooden bungalows and tents every summer. It was called Orchard Beach. However, when Parks Commissioner Robert Moses filled in Pelham Bay and connected the shores of Hunter Island with Rodman's Neck, those who used to return each year were discouraged from doing so and the newly created sandbank was given the name of the former bungalow colony. Nevertheless, lying on the creamy sand of this new public beach and watching the waters lap the shoreline had its own rewards.

If natural shorelines were not your fancy, there were several pools, both public and private. Perhaps the best known public pool was built in Crotona Park in the 1930s alongside Fulton Avenue. But there was always Cascades on 168th Street and Jerome Avenue and the Metropolitan Pool near the Whitlock Avenue subway station. There were others which had been available in the 1920s but which by the 1930s had disappeared. The Starlight Amusement Park near West Farms Square had a huge swimming pool. It seemed that hundreds could be in it at one time. The Clason Point Amusement Park at the end of Soundview Avenue featured a pool whose water was taken right from the neighboring East River. Because there was no filtration system, it was not exactly clean water and it was nicknamed "The Inkwell."

There were also places which were off-limits to swimming but that were used anyway. The small reservoir near Bainbridge Avenue and 208th Street was a nice place to swim, until it was drained and changed into Williamsbridge Oval Park. Only a new, small wading pool in the park was provided to allay the effects of the heat. Farther south, in Hunts Point, the rotting Tiffany Street Pier was a fine jumping off spot, at least until it was refurbished for use in World War II.

Water could also be used for fishing and, if you did not have a fancy fishing rod and all the fixings, an old broomstick and a cord with a bent pin attached, at the end of which was a wriggling worm dug up from a nearby park or empty lot, would do. Fine fishing was to be had where Spuyten Duyvil Creek meets the Hudson in Riverdale. The shoreline of Clason Point was another good spot for casting. City Island was an attraction for all weekend fishermen, and those who could afford it could rent a boat along the Bronx River and take it out to Long Island Sound for some deep water fishing.

When night fell, it was nice to go out with neighborhood friends to an empty lot. There, all would gather some wood and dig a hole. A fire would be lit, and some potatoes roasted in it. These roasted "mickies," as we used to call them, were delicious. At other times, we would put marshmallows at the end of a stick and roast them over the open fire. The gathering would sing or talk over the experiences of the day, enjoying each other's company in simple pleasure.

In the day, for a good time, the amusement parks were available. Starlight Park was the big one. It had a small roller coaster and a carnival atmosphere, besides its huge swimming pool. An early submarine was also on display there for the inspection of patrons. It was a fine place and, if you knew how to do it, you could cling along the east bank of the Bronx River below West Farms Square and find a small hole in the fence where you could sneak in. Of course, this would not enable you to see any attractions at the Colosseum on the amusement park's grounds. Often inside the Colosseum there would be a musical performance or a boxing or wrestling match.

There were other ways to divert yourself as well, and some of these were free. The Goldman Band, for many years, gave free concerts on the New York University campus near the Hall of Fame. On a given Sunday, a band also would be playing in the bandshell in Poe Park.

Most performances had to be paid for, however. The cheapest kind were the fundraising events for the churches or synagogues in each neighborhood. For a modest contribution, a musical revue, a fashion show, or a film could be enjoyed. Parties, such as a strawberry festival, might be thrown in order to raise needed funds. A dance for the young men and women of the congregation would be offered as another fund-raiser, as well as giving the youngsters an opportunity to become acquainted in a supervised social situation.

On rainy days, or in the evening, even the home could be a place of amusement, especially if you listened to the radio. In the early 1920s most of what you would receive over the static-filled airwaves was Hawaiian music, but as more stations got on the air the variety of programming increased. No matter what station you tuned to, whether it was WJZ, WABC, WEAF, WOR, or some other one, each had comedy, music, news, and drama built into its schedule. Arthur Godfrey hosted an early variety show, and he never lost his popularity. However, during the daytime, when he was on, the airwaves were dominated by the soap operas, such as "The Romance of Helen Trent" or "Mary Noble: Backstage Wife." "Aunt Jenny" was an unusual program, combining the standard soap opera story with a segment on recipes to prepare tasty dishes. By late afternoon, the children's shows predominated. "Tom Mix," "Jack Armstrong: The All-American Boy," and "The Adventures of Superman" were some of the shows that appealed to the after-school crowd. The evening was the time for such great comedians as Jack Benny and Fred Allen, and such comedy shows as "Fibber McGee and Molly" and "Amos 'n' Andy." Radio drama was absorbing, especially the mystery shows such as "Inner Sanctum," which always opened with the sound of a creaking door. During the weekends, there were special shows. "Let's Pretend" was a fantasy show for children, but "Grand Central Station" was a genuine drama centering about travelers who came to New York by way of the famous terminal. There was also broadcasts of the Metropolitan Opera and the NBC Symphony Orchestra directed by Arturo Toscanini, and there were such popular music shows as "The Make-Believe Ballroom."

For those of us who lived in The Bronx then, there were two special things about radio. The first was WBNX, the borough's own radio station, which broadcasted out of Starlight Park until it was forced to move when the Depression hit and the amusement park had to close forever. The other was the program "The Goldbergs," starring Gertrude Berg as Molly Goldberg, the warm Jewish mother of a growing household in a really non-existent apartment house on Tremont Avenue. Each story always revolved around some form of normal family crisis, which somehow was solved with dispatch and good humor by the lovable Molly before a half hour had passed. For us in the beautiful Bronx, and for others who heard the program throughout the nation, she symbolized the borough.

If somehow the radio was broken, there was always the phonograph. If you could get a younger brother or sister to constantly crank up the mechanism whenever the turntable was winding down, you could invite some friends over, put on some records, and dance in your own home.

But if anyone would ask you what the most popular entertainment was, the answer was simple. It was the movies. And everybody saw them.

In the 1920s the films were silent, and the showing was accompanied by a piano player during the day and by a full orchestra at night. Those seeing an evening performance, consequently, had to pay a higher admission price to cover the extra cost. When sound films came in, the two-price policy remained, even though there was no real rationale for it. Somehow, nobody complained.

Most of the theaters began in the 1920s as vaudeville houses, and families would go to Keith's Royal Theatre, for instance, to see a complete vaudeville card, which might feature Belle Baker singing "My Yiddishe Momma" or Ernest Truex in a dramatic sketch. Several houses featured both a film and a vaudeville act, especially when sound films began. Ed Sullivan brought his revue to the RKO Chester near West Farms Square. But the Depression forced even these to disappear and the movie theaters in The Bronx showed double features instead.

In those days, to go to a movie theater meant more than seeing a show. In a sense it was going to a world that seemed forbidden, a world of fantasy and of fabulous wealth. The movie houses were not only large, but highly ornate. Lobbies had to be covered with plush carpets bearing intricate designs, and mezzanines outside of rest rooms had to have matching carpets and overstuffed furniture, lamps, vases, heavy carved tables, and paintings hanging from brocaded walls. Inside the auditorium itself, sconces were dimly lit to help you find the way to your seat, and draperies were hung from boxes in the upper level. Giant crystal chandeliers were hung from the ceiling. With these appointments, you were not in a movie theater, but in a palace.

The summit of all the movie palaces in The Bronx was, without doubt, the Loew's Paradise Theatre. Located on the Grand Concourse just south of 188th Street, its facade proclaimed its difference from the ordinary to the world. Alone of all theaters, the Paradise had no marquee overhanging the sidewalk to announce the titles of the movies it was showing. The sign with the movable white letters on a blue background was flush against the wall. Above was a clock surmounted by a huge statue of St. George slaying the dragon. Whenever the hour struck, the statue became animated, the horse heaving up to allow his sainted passenger to slay the snarling beast crouched at his heels. After buying a ticket at the box office, uniformed ushers would sweep you into an anteroom from which cages hung bearing stuffed birds of paradise. Another usher would take your ticket to admit you into a lobby designed to strike any viewer with its opulence. A carved marble fountain was featured on one wall, and goldfish swam in its basin. Above it was a gallery of arched false windows with the glass replaced by mirrors to reflect the plush balcony level. The walls leading to the auditorium were paneled with mahogany wood from which were hung ornately framed reproductions of famous paintings. The ceiling was carved, and embedded in it were paintings such as would be seen in a European palace. More surprises met the viewer once he entered the 4,000-seat auditorium. Here was no ordinary room. It was a vast fantasy-land that resembled an Italian baroque garden. Not only were the walls carved with columns and imitation Michelangelo statuary, but the ceiling was painted blue to resemble a night sky, with pinpoints of light embedded in it to resemble stars that twinkled, and over it all floated puffs of wispy clouds which actually moved across the heavens. The Paradise Theatre was aptly named.

Of course, not all theaters were as large as the Paradise, and not all were decorated in the same manner. In general, in the 1930s, movie houses were made smaller, and the Art Deco design predominated. The Earl Theatre on 161st Street near Yankee Stadium, for instance, had two silhouette statues dimly lit from the rear in niches flanking the stage, and the sconces on the walls were oblong glass coverings with vertical glass fluting which dispersed the dim light emanating from the green colored light bulbs it masked.

Moreover, not all theaters were known for their opulence or modern Art Deco elegance. The Interborough Theatre on Tremont Avenue in Throgs Neck was a notorious spot in the 1920s. Patrons of this movie house almost invariably came back scratching. The theater was infested with lice, and the children of the area aptly called it "The Itch." Luckily, this situation did not exist in most other movie houses.

Movies had a definite round to make when they played in The Bronx. After completing its Broadway run, a film would open up in The Bronx in a first-run theater, such as the Loew's Paradise or the RKO Fordham. When it finished its engagement there, it would be sent to theaters scattered throughout the various Bronx neighborhoods for a second run. Once the film played there, usually for only five days, it was sent to a third-run house. People who lived near 167th Street and the Grand Concourse knew that they could go to the Paradise to see a first-run film, but that if they missed it, it would be nearby at the Loew's 167th Street Theatre in two weeks. It was one of life's sureties.

Once a film had completed its course in The Bronx, there might still be an opportunity to see it again at any one of the theaters which received films by a haphazard schedule and which often showed movies that were several years old. The Fleetwood Theatre at Morris Avenue near 165th Street and the Zenith on 170th Street near Jerome Avenue specialized in these. Often these movie houses were not as filled as the others and not as well maintained.

But it was the movies that we came to see. In general, the films had as much relation to reality as the decor of the theater, but that did not matter, since the movies were an escape from the everyday world for us. It did not matter that Fred Astaire and Ginger Rogers danced over a polished floor in a living room almost as large as an entire apartment house. It was fun.

All but one theater eliminated the stage shows for double feature movies. The lone holdout was the Windsor Theatre on Kingsbridge Road near the spot where it entered Fordham Road. Here were live stage presentations, usually a revival of a Broadway play or musical.

But for those of us who lived in the beautiful Bronx, movies were also a live experience. Along 176th Street near Prospect Avenue was a fence standing beyond the chestnut trees on the sidewalk. Behind the fence was the back lot of the Biograph studios, where several silent films were made in the 1920s. If you waited, you could see such stars as Milton Sills or Bessie Love, or sometimes watch an entire scene being filmed with scores of extras dressed in exotic Spanish costumes.

Of course, such filmwork could not be done in the cold of winter when snow was on the ground. That was the time for other kinds of fun. Snow was always an opportunity for children because it could be fashioned into so many things. Packing a handful into a tight, round snowball was easy, and it was fun to hurl one at your friends. With a large snowfall, mounds of the frosty white stuff could be heaped up next to a curb and a fort fashioned. When a similar fortress was built across the street, the two sides manning the barricades would fling snowballs at each other furiously until all were exhausted. Those with an artistic sense could try to build a snowman. If you had a sled, the nearest snow-covered hill, no matter how slight the slope, could be used for "belly-whopping," flinging yourself on the sled face forward as you started your run down the hill.

Of course, many of the hills in the western part of The Bronx were ideal for this enterprise. A pile of ashes discarded from the coal furnace of a nearby apartment house spread over the end of the course would prevent you from barreling into oncoming traffic at the bottom of the hill. If ashes could not be found, then a friend stationed there could signal you when the coast was clear and no car was in sight. In the Tremont area, 172nd Street between Third and Fulton Avenues, and 174th Street and Anthony Avenue were used. In nearby Belmont, 187th Street and Hughes Avenue served the purpose. In West Farms, the slope at 178th Street and Bryant Avenue was a fine hill, but the hill inside Crotona Park at Crotona Park East was, no doubt, safer. However, coasting a sled down a hill was never confined to those neighborhoods. Folks in Wakefield tried St. Owen Place near Baychester Avenue, and in Soundview, Elder Avenue at Westchester Avenue was a spot for sledding.

With the coming of spring, the snow would melt, but there were new opportunities for diversion. In June every year throughout the 1920s, there was the Bronx Borough Day parade up the Grand Concourse. Every school, whether public or parochial, would contribute a contingent. With all clothes neat and clean, and with school bands in bright uniforms and brass bands playing, the parade would march up the tree-lined boulevard, each participant proud to represent his school and proud to be a Bronxite.

The Borough Day parades ended in the 1930s, but those living along the Grand Concourse never lacked for parades. Memorial Day always had the big one, with all the veterans' groups combining their efforts to produce a big turnout. During World War II, the parade swelled with the current men in uniform adding their numbers to the marchers.

Certainly these were diversions, and they were all a part of the beautiful Bronx. But the center of it all was the home and the family and the very real concerns of life.

V

Hearth and Home

Home, to anyone who lived in The Bronx, had a variety of meanings. To a Riverdalian, it might mean his mansion; to a person from Edgewater Park on Throgs Neck, it might mean his weatherproofed bungalow; to a Clason Point farmer, it could mean his farmhouse; to a resident of Alexander Avenue in Mott Haven, it was his red-brick, brownstone-shaped, attached townhouse; to a Williamsbridge resident, it was his simple wooden frame house; to those who lived along Commonwealth Avenue, it was the two-family house; to some who lived along the shoreline at Ferry Point or Castle Hill, it was the boathouse; and to the lighthouse keeper at Fort Schuyler, it was his lighthouse. But most Bronxites lived in apartment houses.

There were apartment houses in The Bronx before the 1920s began, of course. Marked by their cornices at the roof line, these walk-up apartments had rooms that faced the front, and others that faced the back. Since they were all attached, the chances were very good that just about every apartment had at least one window that faced an air shaft, which was so narrow that you could shake hands with your neighbor standing in the window across the way.

The apartment houses built in the 1920s, however, had more amenities than the earlier ones. The six-story ones had elevators and the elevator operator could be a help in so many ways, especially if a mother was overburdened carrying packages from a store. The entrances were marked by deep and wide courts which sometimes contained shrubs and which often were decorated with stone statues of lions, usually awake and on guard, or sometimes dozing. Flower urns were another decorative device. But the building itself was decorated with jutting brickwork that subtly changed the surface level of the building so that there would be slight shadows on the otherwise flat facade. Whole buildings would be decorated in a Moorish motif or a Spanish colonial or Tudor style. The apartments were generally larger than in the older houses, and moldings decorated the walls.

In the 1930s, most of the apartment houses put up were in the new modern style called Art Deco. Abstract geometric designs could be seen everywhere on these buildings. Cream-colored brick made the facade lighter than the 1920s apartments and contrasting color brick formed all sorts of pleasing abstract designs on the exterior. The entrance was made of concrete forming a geometrical design and iron railings were made to harmonize with it. Inside the lobby, an inlaid floor also contained such abstract designs and often murals were painted on the walls. The lobby was lit with indirect lighting. The apartments had casement windows, and a corner room had the windows located right at the junction of the two walls. A noted feature that anyone who visited an Art Deco apartment immediately noticed was the sunken living room. Two or three steps had to be taken to descend into the living room from the foyer.

No matter what kind of apartment house you lived in, the one advantage was not taking care of the boiler or repairs. That was left to the superintendent. It was he who made sure that the coal was delivered on time, and it was he who stoked it in the furnace, taking out the ashes and storing them in cans until the sanitation men came to pick them up. If a sink was dripping, he would come up to repair it. That was living!

All that service was yours for only about thirty or forty dollars a month in rent for a three-room apartment. Furthermore, landlords were so anxious to get tenants that they offered concessions. Often they would offer you one or two months rent free, a newly painted apartment, and a new refrigerator and stove if you would just sign a lease. As it was, moving from apartment to apartment was a fairly common happening. Once a lease ran out (and they all seemed to expire in October) you simply found another landlord who would offer you similar concessions to sign a lease for one of his apartments, and you moved. Of course, your former landlord would try to find someone else for the one you vacated by offering his new tenant other concessions. In this manner, many Bronx families played musical apartments.

For the housewife and mother, the center of her activity was the kitchen. There, with her gas stove started by lighting a match, she could cook her specialties, whether it was corned beef and cabbage, spaghetti al dente, or latkes. As part of the unit, there was the oven right next to the stove burners, rising from the burner level so that the harassed housewife did not have to bend down to see how her roast was doing. The gas refrigerator was set to work by igniting a pilot light beneath. Electric refrigerators were usually marked by the circular unit on the top.

Of course, no housewife remained in the home. There was shopping to do. No matter what neighborhood you happened to be in, there always seemed to be a shopping street within walking distance. For Highbridge, it was Ogden Avenue; for University Heights, it was University Avenue; for the Grand Concourse, there were several streets, such as 161st Street, 167th Street, 170th Street, Burnside Avenue, 188th Street, and Kingsbridge Road. Mott Haven had 138th Street, and Hunts Point had Southern Boulevard. Those in East Morrisania shopped along Freeman Street, while those in Soundview were attracted to Westchester Avenue. The length of Tremont Avenue serviced all the neighborhoods it touched. Those who lived in the Kingsbridge area shopped at 231st Street, while White Plains Road was the main shopping area for those in the Pelham Parkway, Williamsbridge, and Wakefield neighborhoods.

Nevertheless, there were places that had isolated shops to serve emergency needs. The small center at 165th Street west of the Grand Concourse, for instance, had some grocery stores, a kosher delicatessen, a kosher butcher, a shoemaker, a pharmacy, a vegetable store, a barber shop, a beauty parlor, a Chinese hand laundry, and a candy store, where school supplies, comic books, newspapers, and sodas could be bought, as well as candy.

No matter where the shopping was done, it seemed that it was done in the same way. The grocery store, for instance, was packed to the ceiling with goods stacked on the shelves. The grocer, standing behind the counter, would take the order item by item and fetch it. If it was located on the top shelf, he would take a long pole, at the end of which were two stiff steel bands at right angles to the pole acting like calipers when the grocer pressed a lever. Using this device, he would grab the product requested and bring it down from its high perch. At the end, he would total the entire order on a paper bag, using a pencil, and then place what was ordered in the same bag. The local butcher would do the same thing, and so would the pharmacist.

There were not many supermarkets in those days. Even the A&P, the only large chain, had small stores, and they resembled the local grocery. You could walk into one, and the moment you stepped on the wooden floor, the aroma of freshly ground coffee hit you. That was what the A&P was famous for. On order, you could get a fresh bag of coffee made from beans ground before your eyes.

Some of the larger shopping streets, such as Tremont Avenue between Webster Avenue and Third Avenue, or 138th Street, might attract people from outside the neighborhood, for here were dress shops and furniture stores, as well as the shops for local needs.

But major shopping was done at the Hub. Here were the large department stores gathered under the shadow of the Third Avenue El. The Adams-Flanagan of the 1920s might become a branch of Hearn's in the 1930s, but the bustle of the street never ceased. Great furniture stores, such as Piser's, Ludwig-Baumann's, and Sachs Quality, were there amid the specialty shops. When Alexander's opened there in 1928, the crowds increased. This was the major shopping district in The Bronx and thousands came each day by el, subway, or trolley to shop. At Christmastime, mothers felt compelled to bring their children to the Hub to sit on the lap of the department store Santa.

If the Hub was the major commercial center, Fordham Road was growing into one. Roger's Department Store at Third Avenue was a landmark, but things really began to grow when Alexander's opened its branch store on the Grand Concourse in the old Adams-Wertheimer store and remodeled it. In the 1930s, it boasted that it had more sales per square foot than any other store in the world. Between the two giants, there grew a string of clothing stores, shoe stores, and other shops to entice the buyer.

Oddly, a housewife or a mother did not have to go very far to do much of her shopping in those days. Often the stores came to the door. Vegetable peddlers would come in a horse-drawn wagon, and neighborhood housewives would gather around to select the best cabbage, cucumbers, or tomatoes from the fresh, crisp produce. At other times, there would be a similar wagon selling ice cream pops, and all the children would ask that money be thrown down to them from the apartment house windows above so that they could enjoy a treat. Similar wagons would be sent out by laundries to pick up and deliver their loads. Ice men would go through the streets in such wagons as well, usually delivering to fish stores and other commercial establishments. But the driver would stop on being hailed to sell a cake of ice to anyone whose refrigerator was temporarily broken. Without a wagon, but simply on foot, an old man with his whetstone on his back would travel through the streets announcing that he sharpened knives. Another with a bundle thrown over his shoulder would shout that he bought old clothes.

In a similar manner, entertainment came to the door as well. In the 1940s there was one man who had rigged up his truck with a small merry-go-round, and he would go from neighborhood to neighborhood in warmer weather charging little boys and girls a small fee to ride on his delicately carved horses while music played. He was obviously Irish, since the top of the turning merry-go-round sported green flags with a golden harp. On foot came a random street singer, who would raise his voice in song either on the street or in the back alley. Gearing his songs to the ethnic makeup of the neighborhood, he subsisted on the coins the appreciative audience in the apartments threw down to him.

Of course, the man of the house was more concerned with the prospect of raising the money to pay for the rent and the items bought, and for this he had to work. Most men streaming out of their apartment houses every weekday would take the trolley, bus, or subway and go to Manhattan to work. A select few worked in The Bronx. Some, of course, owned the shops that the women of the borough patronized. Others might work for some of the big firms established in the borough. In Port Morris, the R. Hoe and Company plant, where printing presses and saws were put together, employed thousands of people. In Hunts Point, the American Bank Note Company printed stock certificates and foreign postage stamps. Sometimes the guards there would have to shoo away wise-cracking neighborhood children asking for a sample of foreign currency in which the company specialized. In Highbridge, the H. W. Wilson Company, maker of indexes, was important, and its lighthouse on the roof marked the site of its printing plant. In Mott Haven, the Art Steel Company made steel files painted green. There were other places, whether they were factories, warehouses, or offices, where a man could be employed. He could be pumping gas into a truck at a filling station, or he could be driving the truck. He could be working for a private employer, or he could be a civil servant pounding a beat in a uniform, waiting for an alarm in a firehouse, or approving forms in the borough president's office.

Wherever he worked, he and his wife shared responsibilities for the home, the children, the neighborhood, and the church or synagogue. Certainly, each parent took an active interest in the education of his child and membership in the school's PTA was important to make contact with the teachers and to know what was happening in the school. The religious education of the youngster was important, too. Jewish parents would beam as their son read from the holy scriptures, the Torah, for the first time during the Bar Mitzvah ceremony. Catholic parents had to dress their child in the finest of clothes for First Communion. Both ceremonies marked the passage of time, the coming of age, and acceptance into the religious life.

Of course, the survival of the church or synagogue was also important. Whatever the group was called, be it the Holy Name Society, the Sisterhood, or the Men's Club, the money that it raised was always put to a worthwhile purpose.

But religious groups were not the only ones a person could join. There were clubs and fraternal groups all over the borough. The Schnorer Club had its headquarters on 163rd Street just east of Third Avenue, and the Elks occupied a venerable building at the corner of the Grand Concourse and Burnside Avenue, which was marked by the elk's head overhanging the rounded corner near the roof. The headquarters for the Masons was on Washington Avenue just south of Tremont Avenue. Businessmen were attracted to the service clubs, such as the Lions, the Rotary, and the Kiwanis. They always met in the plush Concourse Plaza Hotel on the Grand Concourse and 161st Street. This social center of The Bronx not only catered to their weekly luncheons, but also served as the locale for political meetings and the swankiest social occasions. At the Hibernian Club-house in Highbridge on 166th Street off Ogden Avenue, the Irish would gather together, while Jews were attracted to the B'nai B'rith or the Zionist Organization of America.

Of course, if anyone in the family fell ill, money for doctors and medicine became a major worry. A doctor would be found in his office in the neighborhood at specified hours, but, at other times, he would make his rounds to the homes of his patients who were bedridden. He would charge a dollar more for a home visit, but he was well prepared with all of his necessary equipment stored in his little black valise he always carried with him. Out of it would pop his stethoscope, tongue depressors, a light for looking at the inner ear, an assortment of pills, a syringe, and other varieties of medical equipment.

If the situation was an emergency and the doctor could not be contacted in time, the ailing patient could always be rushed to the clinic at a nearby hospital. In Hunts Point, Lincoln Hospital was a massive complex to serve the area. On 167th Street between Walton and Gerard Avenues, Morrisania Hospital provided medical care. Its tall smokestack pierced the sky above it. Bronx Hospital rose above Fulton Avenue and 169th Street, while Montefiore Hospital occupied Gun Hill Road near Bainbridge Avenue. Another large hospital, the Kingsbridge Veterans Hospital, occupied nice wooded grounds on Kingsbridge Road between University and Sedgwick Avenues, but it served only the needs of veterans. These were the large hospitals, but there were many throughout The Bronx which were smaller, and they also served the families in the neighborhood. Lebanon Hospital, for instance, occupied an old red-brick building with a mansard roof on a hill overlooking Cauldwell Avenue at Westchester Avenue, and Prospect Hospital was at Kelly and 156th Streets. St. Joseph's Hospital on St. Ann's Avenue was known to give superior medical care. Calvary Hospital on Macombs Road near Featherbed Lane occupied green grounds covered with trees hidden behind a high wall. This institution took in only terminally ill patients. Parkchester General Hospital at Westchester Avenue and Parker Street served the growing Parkchester and Westchester Square neighborhoods. Of course, there were many other hospitals to which a patient could be sent.

With all the activity on behalf of the family and neighborhood going on, naturally there were times when the family would leave the house to relax. Going to a restaurant was an occasion to get away from it all. Although there were places to eat in every neighborhood, there were some special restaurants. In the 1920s, several fine eating establishments, even Chinese restaurants, offered music with the meal. The High Mandarin on Third Avenue and 149th Street was one of these, and so was the Bronx Tea Garden near the Prospect Avenue subway station. The Fordham Casino at Fordham Road and Belmont Avenue featured Italian cuisine, which was to be expected in that Italian neighborhood. Sormani's at Pelham Parkway and White Plains Road was locally famous for the quality of its fare. In the Morris Park area stood the Woodmansten Inn, a roadhouse whose fame reached beyond the bounds of The Bronx. Thwaites on City Island specialized in fresh seafood. There were many others.

However, when the Depression of the 1930s hit, many of these restaurants were forced to go out of business or to eliminate the live orchestras in order to survive. So tight was the dollar that cafeteria eating became popular. Here you could get the food yourself at a steam table, presenting the server behind the counter with a printed ticket on which he punched out the price of the food you had taken. You had to pay the cashier whatever price had been punched on the ticket. The food may not have been as well prepared as in a regular restaurant, nor were the surroundings as elegant with no tablecloths or waiters, but the food was hot and tasty and inexpensive. In the Depression, such cafeterias thrived. The Jerome Cafeteria on 161st Street was across from Yankee Stadium. The 167th Street Cafeteria established itself between River and Gerard Avenues. Bickford's on Fordham Road was very popular. On 170th Street near Walton Avenue was a Horn and Hardart Automat, where you needed nickles to get your food from shelves located behind little glass doors. Its vegetables and coffee were renowned.

For a special treat, there were the ice cream parlors. Of course, the neighborhood candy store could always prepare an ice cream soda or a sundae, but somehow it had a different and creamier taste when it was done in an ice cream parlor. Jahn's on Kingsbridge Road was one such place. Krum's on the Grand Concourse south of Fordham Road was another. A third was Addie Vallin's on 161st Street just across the thoroughfare from the Jerome Cafeteria.

Another way to get away from it all was to go on a little excursion on a Sunday. Usually this meant going down to Manhattan by subway train to visit a museum or see a special movie. However, if a neighbor or a relative had a car, and if he were going into the country, he might bring you and your family along. A pleasant ride was along the Bronx River Parkway. Entering at Southern Boulevard just north of Fordham Road, the roadway wended its way through the beautiful grounds of the Botanical Garden and along the east bank of the Bronx River until it recrossed it at the bridge at 233rd Street. It then continued northward into Westchester County. Another pleasant excursion was to take the Clason Point Ferry across the East River to North Beach in Queens and to continue out to Long Island. The only drawback was the possibility of waiting a long time for the ferry.

The ride to Long Island was greatly shortened in the 1930s with the building of the Triborough Bridge and, later, of the Bronx-Whitestone Bridge, which replaced the Clason Point Ferry. Although now the journey was quicker and somewhat more spectacular since the roadway was raised high over the water, somehow it did not seem the same as being closer to the waves.

Together, all the effort to keep house and home together, to contribute to religious life, and to strengthen the neighborhood brought children to respect their parents and their surroundings. It helped make the atmosphere steady and stable. And it was good that this was so because there were many changes going on in the beautiful Bronx.

VI

Growth and Change

Chronicling the change through the years was the Bronx **Home News,** a daily newspaper that almost everyone read. It was delivered to the door every afternoon by a newsboy, who also collected the money for it each week. The paper was full of interesting and reliable information about all the happenings in The Bronx. Here we could read about a neighbor's wedding or a birth in a family we knew. By reading the **Home News** we learned of the church socials, the political meetings, and the affairs of the day right in our own neighborhood. In this full-sized newspaper, The Bronx was the center of the world.

The **Home News** constantly informed us of the growth in The Bronx. From it, we learned that many streets unpaved in the early 1920s were rapidly being paved, and we discovered that empty lots were being sold for building apartment houses, or new schools to accommodate the hordes of children who would come with their parents to The Bronx. We read about new red and green traffic light systems being installed, and their locations. We knew that Manhattan College was building its new campus in Riverdale, and that nearby some land was sold to develop a suburban community of single family houses called Fieldston.

Fieldston was not the only new neighborhood to arise in the 1920s. There was also the Amalgamated Houses at Sedgwick Avenue and Mosholu Parkway. These walkup apartment houses heralded a new idea when they opened in 1927. Sponsored by Sidney Hillman's Amalgamated Clothing Workers Union, these were the first cooperative apartment houses in New York State. The families would own stock in the cooperative and, in effect, be their own landlords. The idea proved attractive to many members of the union and to their friends and families. Most of the people who moved into these houses, located in a neighborhood that was predominantly Irish, were Jews. In addition to the houses, a cooperative store was established in the basement, where the customers could buy a share of the enterprise and own part of the business. Through the years, more buildings were added nearby and, in time, a special bus was obtained to run between the Amalgamated Houses and the Mosholu Parkway station of the Jerome Avenue subway. Later it continued on to the Bedford Park Boulevard station of the Concourse line, where the clothing workers could get the "C" Express train to the garment district on Eighth Avenue.

Of course, the 1920s also witnessed the time of Prohibition, but no one could slacken the thirst of hearty Bronxites. Despite all the encouragement to drink such things as U-No-Us, the soda produced by the Bruckner Brothers, and near beer, a request at an old saloon for a "sarsaparilla" with a knowing wink would produce the real thing. In turn, this was produced by "the Bronx Beer Baron," "Dutch" Schultz, and those in the know were aware that he made his headquarters in an office building on 149th Street near Third Avenue.

As more people poured into the new Bronx apartment houses, traffic had a tendency to increase and some of the main streets had to be widened. Several apartment houses and taxpayers, for instance, had to be destroyed when Boscobel Avenue was made double its previous size. Later, in the 1930s, Mott Avenue was widened and the name of the Grand Concourse was assigned to it to carry that great boulevard south from 161st Street, where it had once begun, to 138th Street. In the mid-1940s, Eastern Boulevard, by then called Bruckner Boulevard, was also widened, with traffic islands added.

In the 1930s, the biggest fact of life was the Great Depression. With the plummeting prices, many businesses went under and unemployment was widespread. It was common for neighbors to inquire if your father was still working. It became a struggle for many Bronx families to provide the needed food and clothing. Raising the money to pay the rent was a chore. Over all hung the possibility that the landlord might evict the entire family, leaving everyone surrounded by furniture on an empty sidewalk. Many had to swallow their pride and accept charity for the first time in their lives, and later, when it became available, Home Relief. It was not pleasant, but the family survived.

In desperation, most Bronxites turned to President Franklin D. Roosevelt as if to a savior, and those who read the **Home News** knew that one of the President's major backers was Edward J. Flynn, the Democratic boss of the borough. In the 1930s, many government public works projects rose in The Bronx because of Ed Flynn, and those who realized it blessed him for it. The new post office on the Grand Concourse at 149th Street, the new Bronx County Jail south of Yankee Stadium, and the conversion of Williamsbridge Reservoir into a park were all done by agencies of the federal government, providing needed jobs. The local Democratic clubs took care to see to the needs of Bronxites. The Star Democratic Club in Hunts Point hosted the neighborhood children every Saturday and gave them free hot dogs. The Sedgwick Democratic Club in Highbridge was filled every night with neighborhood residents asking for favors, and the favors were granted.

For all this, most Bronxites were grateful. At election time, the local district captain would come to the door, reminding everyone that the election was coming and that all the adults should register to vote. He would come again on election day to remind the adults to go to the polls and vote the straight Democratic ticket. Most Bronxites needed no reminding of the favors given to them, and year after year the Democratic label assured any candidate of a landslide victory.

Certainly, the one Democratic candidate who won consistently every four years was James J. Lyons, who became the President of the Borough of The Bronx succeeding Henry Bruckner. This jovial man was seen everywhere. He would be at a dedication of a new bridge, a new park, or a new post office. He would attend luncheons and meetings constantly boosting The Bronx as the best place to live. It was he who named The Bronx

"The Borough of Universities." With his warm smile, he became as much a symbol of The Bronx to those who lived there as Molly Goldberg was for those who did not.

It seems that in those years The Bronx got a name throughout the country, and so did the **Home News.** It certainly startled us to learn that our favorite newspaper played a vital part in the events involving the kidnaping of the Lindbergh baby. Once the kidnaper had been arrested, the paper broke the story that John F. Condon, who taught education at Fordham, had used the **Home News** as the medium to contact the kidnaper, and that he had met him at Woodlawn and St. Raymond's Cemeteries. At the trial, Dr. Condon had identified himself as coming from The Bronx, "the most beautiful borough in the world." He did not have to convince us that it was true.

Another event that seemed to focus attention on The Bronx was Franklin Roosevelt's election campaign visit in 1940. Thousands lined the streets on either side of 138th Street as his motorcade drove along. Women burst into applause when he was driven up the Grand Concourse for a reception at Fordham University. It was not usual for a President to visit The Bronx, and all there strained to get a view of a very special man who was, in many respects, their hero.

While The Bronx was getting a nationwide reputation, there was still growth and change. The Metropolitan Life Insurance Company purchased the land on which the Catholic Protectory stood in order to build a large housing development, which it called Parkchester. Tall brick apartment houses were constructed, decorated at points with orange terra-cotta gargoyles, in the midst of wide, tree-lined streets. Along Unionport Road a shopping center was built and shopkeepers began to occupy the stores. Probably the most important store was Macy's, a branch of the large downtown department store. There was also a movie theatre, the Loew's American. Most of those who moved into this instant neighborhood were Irish, and from the beginning the community was close-knit. The oval-shaped park in the center of the complex where Unionport Road met Metropolitan Avenue to form Metropolitan Oval was a popular meeting and resting spot. Its large green fountain with a fat fish spouting water from its mouth provided the added soothing sound of splashing. However, by the time the complex was finished, events of the outside world were not as soothing.

If the overwhelming problem of the 1930s was the Depression, the major event of the 1940s was World War II. People listened with shock as the news of the attack on Pearl Harbor came over their radios into their living rooms. Almost overnight, The Bronx was transformed. Young men could now be seen walking about in khaki uniforms, and there were tearful farewells as loved ones bid the family goodbye for overseas duty. The only ones left at home were schoolchildren, older men, those who had some disability, and those involved with work vital to the war. During the war, The Bronx was dominated by women in the streets, most of whom anxiously awaited the arrival of the mailman each morning and afternoon for a precious letter from a man in uniform. Most of the time, such letters were in the form of V-Mail, a photographic reproduction of the actual letter reduced in size for easier delivery.

On the home front, The Bronx seemed united in an effort to win the war. At City Island, the yacht makers converted their facilities to make PT boats. R. Hoe and Company on 138th Street began manufacturing cannons. Neighbors volunteered for duty as air raid wardens, donning white helmets bearing a blue circle in which was a triangle consisting of diagonal red and white stripes. A white arm band bearing the same insignia completed the costume. On occasion, air-raid drills would be staged, and when the sirens wailed at night, all the lights in the house had to be turned out and the window shades drawn. Woe betide the errant resident who let even one spark of light escape from his window. Everyone felt that he had to do his part, especially in the scrap drives. Metal pots and pans were collected at the local police station so that they could be melted down for war materials.

There were shortages during the war. Items such as sugar, gasoline, and shoes were severely rationed. When buying sugar at the local grocery store, you not only had to pay the price, but a set number of ration stamps had to be torn from a government-issued book. Without these stamps, you could not get the sugar. There were meatless Tuesdays proclaimed because of the shortage of meat. It really was no great sacrifice because meat was very scarce and not much could be bought anyway. Paper was another scarce item, and paper bags that were used to carry items from the grocery store had to be used over and over again until they were torn beyond repair.

A visible sign of the war could be seen at the newly built Hunter College campus at Bedford Park Boulevard and the Jerome Park Reservoir. With the onset of the war, the four Tudor Gothic buildings were turned over to the WAVES as a training station, and it was common to see the women in their naval uniforms marching in drill formation.

Of course, the most common sight during the war was the little white standards bearing blue stars that hung in the windows of those homes which had sent a son to the war. There was one star for each son who went. It was a gesture by which a family could proclaim to the world its contribution to the war effort. If the blue star in the window was replaced by a gold one, everyone in the neighborhood felt sad, for it meant that notice had been received that the young man had been killed in the line of duty, protecting the freedom that we all cherished.

With all the strain and effort that people were under during the war, the announcement of peace was met with great joy and excitement. Dancing in the streets, honking of horns, and block parties at night met the news that the fighting had ended. As the boys came home, they were welcomed with open arms and neighbors were invited into the house to celebrate the return of the war hero.

With the coming of peace, change continued in The Bronx. Hunter College, which had been used by the WAVES during the war, was now turned to the keeping of the peace. The campus was used by the United Nations Security Council for its meetings just after the war, and the marching women were now replaced by Marines running up the flags of the victorious United Nations from the flagpoles implanted around the circular driveway between the Gymnasium Building and Student Hall. It was exciting to watch the delegates arrive to begin their deliberations. There was a euphoric feeling that, perhaps, this time peace would be kept and the nations of the world would work together to ensure it.

When the United Nations left, Hunter College finally returned to claim its campus, but even then change was evident. Hunter was a renowned women's college, but so many servicemen had returned from the war demanding an education that Hunter opened up its Bronx campus to them and Hunter College had male students walking about its grounds for the first time.

The ex-serviceman coming home was burdened with other problems as well. He had to find a place to live, often with a new bride and a beginning family. Since there were plenty of empty lots in Soundview, temporary shelters were erected for them there. These were the quonset huts, long semicircular metal structures. It was difficult to live there, but the new brides tried to make life comfortable by planting some flowers between the concrete walkways connecting the rows of huts.

Of course, the national hero of most Bronxites, Franklin Roosevelt, never lived to see the end of the war, but Boss Ed Flynn felt he had backed a winner when he threw in his lot with the new President, Harry Truman. Once again, a President visited The Bronx.

During his election campaign in 1948, Harry Truman came down the Concourse, speeded along with the aid of a police motorcycle escort with sirens blaring, waving to the assembled crowd (which included children from nearby schools) while sitting atop the folded-down cover of his convertible car. He stopped at the Concourse Plaza Hotel for a luncheon in his honor.

Through all this great change, and the tremendous growth and recognition in The Bronx, the core remained steady. The family, the neighborhood, the schools, and the religious institutions remained unchanged in spirit. However, by 1950, there were more fundamental changes that could be discerned.

Epilogue

Perhaps the first major change of the late 1940s to be felt by all the members of the family was the Bronx **Home News** ceasing publication. Despite the fact that there were several other newspapers published in New York City, that very special newspaper no longer existed to tell us all the very human stories of our neighbors and our neighborhood. It was a grievous loss.

By 1948 the trolley cars ceased to run. Except for a few trolleys which originated in Westchester County (which would also go in a few years), no one could enjoy the smooth rides and the cool summer breezes in the open cars as in the past. Buses replaced the trolleys, but it just was not the same. On some streets the embedded steel rails were torn up, but most often they were left there for a few years, and then covered with asphalt.

By then television was beginning to become a popular form of entertainment. Slowly, television antennae began sprouting on the roofs of apartment houses, which had hitherto been used only as places to string clotheslines for drying wet wash. The first person in the apartment house to buy one of the new, bulky console sets would invite everyone to his home to see a performance of "The Texaco Star Theatre" starring Milton Berle. We would all gather around the set, squeezing into the living room every Tuesday night at eight o'clock to see the show. In atmosphere, it was very much like going to a movie, and the living room was transformed into a theater. But the streets were deserted at that time. Later, first one neighbor, then another, would buy a set, and the group began to break up, each family isolating itself in its own apartment.

In the late 1940s the last farm in The Bronx disappeared, and the remaining empty lots were being taken for further construction. The veterans in their quonset huts and the children who had grown to maturity in the beautiful Bronx had difficulty finding a good place to live since very few apartments were vacant. They were forced to move out of the neighborhood and go elsewhere.

Moreover, with returning prosperity, many believed that it was time to learn to drive and to buy a car. Suddenly, fewer people were riding the subways to work and the sacred nickel fare had to be raised to ten cents. Parking spaces at curbside became more and more scarce, and traffic jams at major intersections became more common. It was much nicer to drive in the open spaces of the country outside of The Bronx than to stay in the increasingly congested city.

In short, what was changing did not reflect a mere alteration in the neighborhood. What was changing was an entire way of life.

It is true that The Bronx of today is different from The Bronx of 1920 to 1950. Change will always occur. Nevertheless, a considerable number of familiar sights have not changed. People are still using the subways to get to work; the Hub and Fordham Road are still thriving shopping centers; the neighborhood groceries and other shops still provide the basic necessities for their customers; the libraries are still dispensing books; the spring flowers still bloom in the Botanical Garden; the feeding time at the Bronx Zoo still attracts the crowds; the Hall of Fame, with more busts than ever before, still has a spectacular view; Edgar Allan Poe's devotees still make their pilgrimage to Poe Cottage; and the Yankees are still winning ball games at Yankee Stadium. In many ways, it is still the beautiful Bronx.

Photo Album

138TH STREET BETWEEN ALEXANDER AND WILLIS AVENUES in about 1946 had older apartments row upon row, their cornices forming almost a single line. The 138th Street Crosstown trolley has stopped to pick up passengers. The Third Avenue elevated structure in the background operates on its own right of way through the backyards of the buildings which flank it.

(Courtesy of The Bronx County Historical Society, New York City)

138TH STREET AND BROOK AVENUE welcomes President Franklin Roosevelt with great acclaim on October 28, 1940. Crowds line the streets, stand on fire escapes, and peer out of windows to catch a glimpse of the President. The older apartment houses attached to each other with the shops at street level can be easily seen.

(Courtesy of The Bronx County Historical Society, New York City)

A HORSE-DRAWN LAUNDRY WAGON awaits the return of the driver on a delivery at 138th Street near Bruckner Boulevard in 1948.

BUILDING THE BRONX APPROACH TO THE TRIBOROUGH BRIDGE in the 1930s led to the destruction of several buildings in its path. Cypress Avenue is the street at the right. The existing bridge to the left carries the New Haven Railroad into Queens.

THE HUB, about 1950, had traffic streaming along 149th Street beneath the Third Avenue El station. Stores flank both sides of the street and office buildings rise above them. Behind the elevated structure is Hearn's Department Store.

(Courtesy of The Bronx County Historical Society, New York City)

THE RKO ROYAL THEATRE on Westchester Avenue near the Hub began as a vaudeville house in the 1920s. By 1931, when this photograph was taken, it had already converted to showing movies.

(Courtesy of The Bronx County Historical Society, New York City)

ST. ANN'S AVENUE JUST SOUTH OF WESTCHESTER AVENUE, about 1950, is a scene of mixed commercial and residential use. Apartment houses, frame houses, shops, and warehouses can be seen. The elevated structure served both the White Plains Road subway line and the Third Avenue El.

149TH STREET AND COURTLANDT AVENUE, about 1950, is dominated by the Busher Building, one of several office buildings west of the Hub. On the street level is one of the many banks that had their Bronx headquarters on 149th Street.

THE NEW YORK CENTRAL TRACKS in the late 1940s carry a streamlined Union Pacific train north of 149th Street along Park Avenue.
(Courtesy of The Bronx County Historical Society, New York City)

THE DEDICATION OF THE BRONX CENTRAL POST OFFICE at the Grand Concourse and 149th Street in the late 1930s. Addressing the crowd is Bronx Borough President James J. Lyons, and the ceremonies are being broadcast by WNYC, New York City's radio station, and the Bronx's own WBNX.

(Courtesy of The Bronx County Historical Society, New York City)

ARCHBISHOP FRANCIS SPELLMAN lays the cornerstone of Cardinal Hayes High School on the Grand Concourse and 153rd Street on November 20, 1940.

(Courtesy of The Bronx County Historical Society, New York City)

161ST STREET AND SHERIDAN AVENUE looking toward the Grand Concourse in the mid-1920s. The Concourse Plaza Hotel rises to the right. The trolley tracks and the overhead wires, which provided the electricity for the trolley cars, descend through the Concourse underpass. The vacant lots to the left are used for billboards, one of which announces the long-running Broadway play **Abie's Irish Rose**. (Courtesy of The Bronx County Historical Society, New York City)

161ST STREET AND WALTON AVENUE, about 1950, has the Bronx County Building dominating the scene. Buses are lined up in front for a civic ceremony. On Walton Avenue can be seen some 1920s apartment houses. Behind them, on Gerard Avenue, a cream-colored Art Deco apartment house can be seen. In the distance is Yankee Stadium. (Courtesy of The Bronx County Historical Society, New York City)

THE GRAND CONCOURSE at 161st Street in 1950. The Bronx County Building dominates the corner at the right. Beyond the neo-classical structure rises Franz Sigel Park, a hilly recreation area with a wide variety of trees. The building above the park to the left with the long windows is one of the many factories in Mott Haven. The others are in nearby Manhattan. The latest model city buses hog the roadway where the Grand Concourse narrows south of 161st Street.

AT THE OPENING OF THE BRONX COUNTY BUILDING, 1934, some of the early workers gather for their photograph to mark the occasion. The men in uniform on the steps of the Grand Concourse entrance operated the elevators. Bronx Borough President James J. Lyons is standing in the front row to the left wearing a derby.

(Courtesy of The Bronx County Historical Society, New York City)

BRONX BOROUGH PRESIDENT JAMES J. LYONS BOOSTS THE RED CROSS, 1944, as part of the war effort. The float stands outside the Bronx County Building on the Grand Concourse. Across the street are the new Art Deco apartment houses built in the late 1930s.

(Courtesy of The Bronx County Historical Society, New York City)

THE CONCOURSE PLAZA HOTEL, the center of Bronx social functions, at the Grand Concourse and 161st Street in the late 1940s flies the flag of the Kiwanis Club beside Old Glory. In the lower left-hand corner, the sign on the sidewalk announces that the Lions Club also meets in the hotel. A small traffic jam is beginning to form at the intersection, presaging greater traffic jams to come. To the left of the hotel is one of the Art Deco apartment houses built along the Grand Concourse. It has a roof penthouse.   (Courtesy of The Bronx County Historical Society, New York City)

MAYOR WILLIAM O'DWYER AND FRANCIS CARDINAL SPELLMAN enter the lobby of the Concourse Plaza Hotel for an important function in the late 1940s.   (Courtesy of The Bronx County Historical Society, New York City)

JAMES J. LYONS WELCOMES PRESIDENT HARRY S. TRUMAN at the Concourse Plaza Hotel during the election campaign of 1948.

BRONX BOROUGH PRESIDENT JAMES J. LYONS ADDRESSES THE BRONX LIONS CLUB at a weekly luncheon in the Concourse Plaza Hotel in 1949.   (Courtesy of The Bronx County Historical Society, New York City)

OPENING OF THE BRONX TERMINAL MARKET on the Harlem River near Yankee Stadium in 1935 brought together Mayor Fiorello LaGuardia (who cut the ribbon), Bronx Borough President James J. Lyons, and Markets Commissioner William Fellowes Morgan, Jr.   (Courtesy of The Bronx County Historical Society, New York City)

THE BRONX COUNTY JAIL UNDER CONSTRUCTION, 1936, with the Bronx Terminal Market to the left and Yankee Stadium to the right. It was being built on River Avenue north of 150th Street as a PWA project.

THE BRONX COUNTY JAIL, 1937, is almost completed. This view from River Avenue north of 150th Street obscures the Bronx Terminal Market behind the structure, but Yankee Stadium can still be seen to the right. The sign over the entrance to the edifice announces that the work was performed by the PWA.

WALTON AVENUE AND 158TH STREET, about 1950, shows a typical 1920s apartment house with a deep court entrance. The metal structures on the roof were meant for the residents to string clothesline rope across to dry their wet wash. A man on the corner leans against the side of the building to gather the warmth of the direct sunlight and the reflected heat from the bricks of the building. (Courtesy of The Bronx County Historical Society, New York City)

OPENING DAY AT YANKEE STADIUM, April 18, 1923, brought crowds to the flag-decked structure and cars were hard-pressed to find a place to park. Few knew then that the Stadium was to become the "Home of Champions."

(Courtesy of The Bronx County Historical Society, New York City)

YANKEE STADIUM DURING THE WORLD SERIES, 1947, is packed with fans. The famed ball park is bedecked with bunting, and American flags fly from the roof flagstaffs instead of the usual team pennants. Sharing the roof with them are the light stanchions which had been installed for night games. The Yankees won the 1947 Series, their 13th World Championship.

(Courtesy of The Bronx County Historical Society, New York City)

MILLER HUGGINS AND JACOB RUPPERT at the opening of Yankee Stadium.

JOE McCARTHY, manager of the New York Yankees during the 1930s, surveys the scene from the Yankee dugout.

JOE DIMAGGIO HOLDS THE HAND OF MRS. BABE RUTH AS JAMES J. LYONS LOOKS ON at the dedication ceremonies of Babe Ruth Plaza in 1949. The Plaza was built at 161st Street near Yankee Stadium.

THE LOEW'S 167TH STREET THEATRE near River Avenue was a movie house in the midst of a local shopping street in 1947. It usually showed films a few weeks after their first run in The Bronx had ended.

MORRISANIA HOSPITAL dominates the corner of 167th Street and Gerard Avenue in about 1950. The huge smokestack which marked the site rises to the right. The smoke to the right of that is really steam coming out of a smaller chimney over the laundry room.

(Courtesy of The Bronx County Historical Society, New York City)

THE GRAND CONCOURSE JUST SOUTH OF 169TH STREET has the sidewalk curb flanked with cars. To the left is the wide court entrance and the shrubbery of a 1920s apartment building. Partially obscured by the edge of the building to the center is the Congregation Adath Israel synagogue. Across 169th Street is an Art Deco apartment house. The leaves of the trees along the boulevard produce welcome shade.

(Courtesy of The Bronx County Historical Society, New York City)

BRONX BOROUGH DAY PARADE, 1928, passes by an apartment house south of 170th Street. Some children watch from a fire escape.

(Courtesy of The Bronx County Historical Society, New York City)

Home for Friendless Children, Bronx, New York

THE HOME FOR FRIENDLESS CHILDREN stood on Woodycrest Avenue on the slope of the steep hill rising above Jerome Avenue. Although the home bore the air of a haughty mansion, the boys who were housed inside were friends with the other children of the neighborhood and often played in the nearby parks.

(Courtesy of The Bronx County Historical Society, New York City)

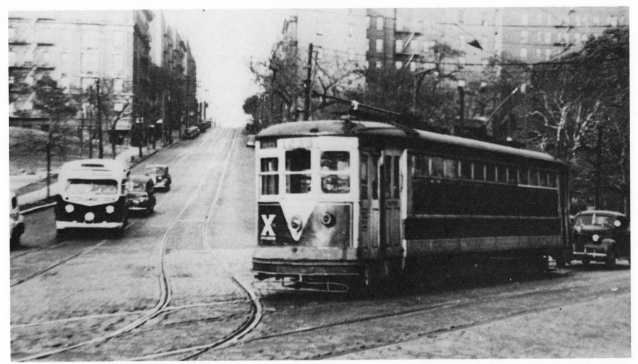

OGDEN AVENUE WHERE IT BEGINS AT JEROME AVENUE in the late 1940s has a bus coming down the steep hill at Ogden Avenue while the 163rd Street crosstown trolley waits on Jerome Avenue. The apartments of Highbridge rise behind the parks at the base of the hill. (Courtesy of The Bronx County Historical Society, New York City)

WOODYCREST AVENUE NEAR 166TH STREET, 1939, was filled with mothers tending their children playing in the street or in baby carriages. Apartment houses built in the 1920s and 1930s dominate the scene, but toward the middle of the photograph can be seen a small taxpayer at the corner of 167th Street. At that corner, a delicatessen, a drug store, a tailor, and other shops serve the people on the street. At the end of the street rises Sacred Heart Church. (Courtesy of The Bronx County Historical Society, New York City)

OGDEN AVENUE NEAR 170TH STREET, 1949, was the northern end of Highbridge's main street. The apartment house to the right has a clothesline strung between windows and wet wash hanging from it. The shops of the street include a kosher delicatessen, a sure sign that Jews live in the neighborhood. The striped pole signals the presence of a barber shop. The curb is crowded with parked cars, including an old station wagon with wooden sides.

THE HIGH BRIDGE, about 1940, was a major walkway for the people of the Highbridge neighborhood into Manhattan across the Harlem River. The sights of northern Manhattan included the towers of the recently completed George Washington Bridge on the horizon.

BOSCOBEL AVENUE BEING WIDENED in the early 1930s. As seen from near Plimpton Avenue, several taxpayers and houses have been destroyed to widen the street. The residents of the apartment house to the left have their awnings drawn to keep out the afternoon sun. The workers are wearing white shirts. In the distance on the horizon is Morrisania Hospital.

(Courtesy of The Bronx County Historical Society, New York City)

BOSCOBEL AVENUE sees a 167th Street Crosstown trolley climbing up the hill toward Washington Bridge in the late 1930s. The trolley's sides have been removed and replaced by an iron mesh fence for summer use.

(Courtesy of The Bronx County Historical Society, New York City)

THE VIADUCT THAT CONNECTS MELROSE AVENUE AND WEBSTER AVENUE over the railroad tracks in 1949 had factories at Webster Avenue. The round milk bottle rises above the Sheffield Farms milk plant.

THE SHEFFIELD FARMS MILK PLANT, about 1950, featured the round milk bottle on the roof, a local landmark. Inside the plant, the milk was poured into bottles, placed on trucks, and sent from the gleaming white building at Webster Avenue and 166th Street to grocery stores throughout The Bronx.

ACME BEER DISTRIBUTORS on Webster Avenue near 170th Street was one of the large number of firms that were established in the single-story taxpayers which flanked the long thoroughfare. Of course, the repeal of Prohibition made beer distribution a thriving business in the 1930s, and Acme sold the suds by the bottle, case, or keg.

(Courtesy of The Bronx County Historical Society, New York City)

THE FRANKLIN THEATRE on Prospect Avenue in 1926 was a vaudeville house on the Keith circuit. It was flanked by neighborhood shops.

THE FRANKLIN THEATRE on Prospect Avenue in 1941 showed double feature movies and was part of the RKO chain. At the tail end of the Depression, a lower admission price at night and cash prizes were awarded to try to attract patrons.

THE LOEW'S BURLAND THEATRE on Prospect Avenue north of 163rd Street was a theatre in the midst of a local shopping street. Located on heavily patronized Prospect Avenue, it was a natural attraction for those seeking entertainment in 1939, when this photograph was taken.

MORRIS HIGH SCHOOL loomed over its surroundings at Boston Road and 166th Street. Rich in Gothic architectural detail, it had the atmosphere of a college. *(Courtesy of The Bronx County Historical Society, New York City)*

THE LOEW'S BOSTON ROAD THEATRE at Boston Road near Wilkins Avenue played the double features usual in Bronx neighborhood houses in 1948. Although located only a block away from spacious Crotona Park, it abutted the local shopping street, where residents could get their hair cut in the barber shop or drop their snapshots off for developing before entering the movie house. *(Courtesy of The Bronx County Historical Society, New York City)*

THE JUNCTION OF 149TH STREET, PROSPECT AVENUE, AND SOUTHERN BOULEVARD, 1921, had the poles holding the overhead wires for the trolleys located in the middle of the street. Empty lots with billboards dominate the corner. One billboard announces the latest vaudeville attraction at the Royal Theatre.

(Courtesy of The Bronx County Historical Society, New York City)

163RD STREET AT TIFFANY STREET, 1949, was lined with shops located at the sidewalk level of the older walk-up apartment buildings. The elevated structure in the background rises over Westchester Avenue.

(Courtesy of The Bronx County Historical Society, New York City)

SOUTHERN BOULEVARD AND AVENUE ST. JOHN, about 1950, was filled with walk-up apartment houses. The ground floor of some of them contained shops which catered to the people living in the neighborhood. A dry cleaner, a dairy and grocery, a Chinese hand laundry, a barber shop, a candy store with a newspaper stand outside, and a hardware store could be seen in many Bronx neighborhoods at that time. The trolley tracks still remain embedded in Southern Boulevard, but the trolley had already been replaced by a bus, whose stop was at the corner.

(Courtesy of The Bronx County Historical Society, New York City)

167TH AND TIFFANY STREETS in the 1940s had an old walk-up apartment house on the corner, elaborately decorated with a cornice near the roof. At the corner was a typical neighborhood grocery store, replete with ads for Coca Cola, Salada Tea, and various brands of beer in the window. On the top floor, a woman looks out the window to the street below, a common practice of many Bronx mothers to keep an eye on their children. On the lamppost is a mailbox of the period.

(Courtesy of The Bronx County Historical Society, New York City)

BRUCKNER BOULEVARD NEAR THE BRONX RIVER in the mid-1940s became a wide tree-lined thoroughfare. However, traffic had to squeeze together to get from Hunts Point in the foreground across the railroad bridge (marked by its steel beam superstructure) and the bridge over the river beyond it to the Soundview section. The forest of apartment houses clusters near the Pelham Bay subway line on Westchester Avenue, which is out of sight. The relatively empty land to the right leads to Clason Point.　　　(Courtesy of The Bronx County Historical Society, New York City)

HOE AVENUE AND JENNINGS STREET in the 1930s witnesses an accident, and the neighbors gather around to find out what happened. A city ambulance has quickly arrived at the scene and the man who was hurt is being carried away to a city hospital.　　　(Courtesy of The Bronx County Historical Society, New York City)

WEST FARMS ROAD NEAR JENNINGS STREET, 1948, contained an automobile repair shop and gas station. Through the alleyway in the center can be seen the Bronx River and the Soundview shore opposite. A tower servicing the nearby New Haven Railroad tracks is at the right.　　　　(Courtesy of The Bronx County Historical Society, New York City)

EDGEWATER ROAD NEAR 172ND STREET in the 1940s was a quiet street on the west bank of the Bronx River in West Farms. A corner gas station is flanked by a row of brick brownstone-type buildings, while in the distance can be seen apartment houses and frame houses.　　　　(Courtesy of The Bronx County Historical Society, New York City)

PROSPECT PLACE BETWEEN CLAY AND ANTHONY AVENUES, about 1950, was a quiet street with small houses. The brick building to the left was a Jewish old folks' home. Beyond the mound and the trees can be seen the apartment houses of the Tremont neighborhood. (Courtesy of The Bronx County Historical Society, New York City)

THE BRONX EYE AND EAR INFIRMARY was a small hospital on Tremont Avenue near Anthony Avenue in the early 1940s. (Courtesy of The Bronx County Historical Society, New York City)

TREMONT AVENUE EAST OF THIRD AVENUE in the 1940s thronged with people on the sidewalks and with trolleys in the streets. The trees to the right form the boundary of that section of Crotona Park also known as Victory Park.

THE BRONX BOROUGH HALL in Crotona Park stood on top of a hill at Third and Tremont Avenues. Until the Bronx County Building was built in the 1930s, this was the center of Bronx civic life. Even afterward, it served as a meeting place for many organizations, and everyone who lived in The Bronx had to apply for his marriage license in this yellow-brick building with its brown terra-cotta trim.   (Courtesy of The Bronx County Historical Society, New York City)

THE FOUNTAIN IN CROTONA PARK near Tremont and Arthur Avenues was surrounded with formal flower plantings flanking the paths that radiated from its base. It was a lovely place in which to stroll in the early 1920s, when the small section behind the Borough Hall was still called Victory Park from the days of World War I. The large building on Arthur Avenue to the right is the Bergen Building, which housed several city offices.

(Courtesy of The Bronx County Historical Society, New York City)

THE LOEW'S FAIRMOUNT THEATRE on Tremont Avenue contained the lavish decorations of most movie houses in the 1920s. With a plush carpeted floor, overstuffed furniture, and flowers filling jars and vases, the mezzanine had the air of an exclusive private club. A cut-glass chandelier and a wall mural completed the spacious and elegant room.

(Courtesy of The Bronx County Historical Society, New York City)

AN AERIAL VIEW OF WEST FARMS in 1949 reveals a forest of apartment houses. The Bronx Zoo is the large park to the right. Near the lower left-hand corner is West Farms Square leading to the West Farms elevated station of the subway. Along the subway line closer to the zoo is the Bronx Zoo station of the Seventh Avenue subway line. One train is pulling out of the station headed toward a rendezvous with the tracks of the Lexington Avenue subway's White Plains line at West Farms Square. Factories can be seen in the lower right-hand corner.

(Courtesy of The Bronx County Historical Society, New York City)

WEST FARMS SQUARE in the late 1930s sees a Tremont Avenue westbound trolley stalled by another trolley ahead of it while an eastbound passenger waits for his trolley to the left. A shop across the street houses a Bickford's cafeteria, one of the more popular chains.   (Courtesy of The Bronx County Historical Society, New York City)

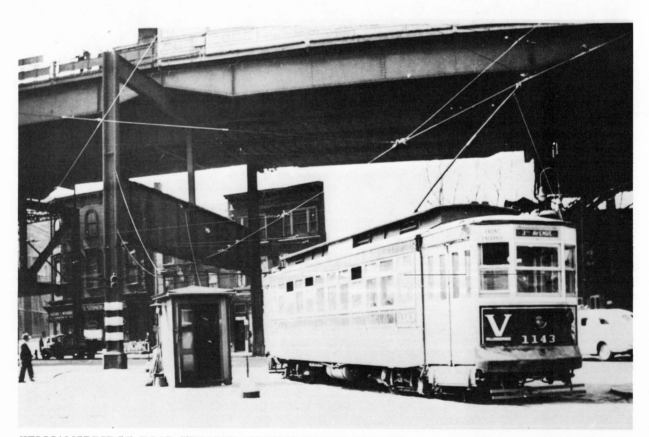

WILLIAMSBRIDGE ROAD TROLLEY AT WEST FARMS SQUARE moves into Boston Road under the West Farms Square station of the White Plains Road subway line in the late 1940s.

(Courtesy of The Bronx County Historical Society, New York City)

WEST FARMS SQUARE, 1948, is the meeting place of the Bronx and Van Cortlandt Parks bus and the Tremont and Williamsbridge trolleys.
(Courtesy of The Bronx County Historical Society, New York City)

THE PARK PLAZA THEATRE stood on University Avenue and Tremont Avenue. This is how it looked on a rainy day in the 1940s. To the right is P.S. 82 at the northern end of McCombs Road, where it entered University. The Park Plaza played movies late in their run and was a fine gathering place for neighborhood children on a day like this. The offices in the building housed the Franklin Roosevelt Chapter of the American Veterans' Committee, a dental laboratory, and a Hebrew school.
(Courtesy of The Bronx County Historical Society, New York City)

UNIVERSITY HEIGHTS FROM THE AIR, 1939, shows a scene dominated by apartment houses and single family homes. The New York University campus is in the center, with the Hall of Fame at the left. Sedgwick Avenue is the street going diagonally to the left between the two large apartment houses and the trees. The parallel street that ends at the campus is Osborne Place. The wide street to the right at the end of the campus grounds is University Avenue. The private houses in the center are between 179th and 180th Streets. Despite the congestion, trees and grass abound in the neighborhood.

(Courtesy of The Bronx County Historical Society, New York City)

THE HALL OF FAME in 1920 dominated the hill that led to the Harlem River valley. At that time, no busts had been set up between the columns.   (Courtesy of The Bronx County Historical Society, New York City)

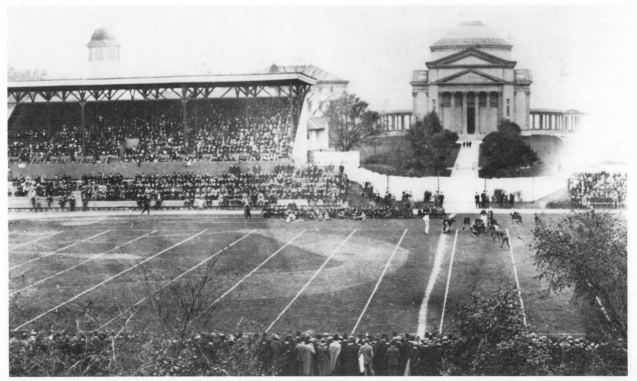

THE NEW YORK UNIVERSITY CAMPUS in 1921 plays host to a football game. The grounds, Ohio Field, were used for baseball as well. The Gould Memorial Library is the building with the rotunda in the rear, and the colonnade behind it is the Hall of Fame.   (Courtesy of The Bronx County Historical Society, New York City)

THE GOLDMAN BAND PLAYS A CONCERT on the campus of New York University in the summer of 1926. The crowd could sit on wooden benches or on the grass. The gabled house with the chimneys near the center is South Hall.

FORDHAM ROAD AND SEDGWICK AVENUE, 1949, is dominated by the construction of the Fordham Hill Houses. The trees mark the site of a park, and playground equipment can be seen to the right.

FORDHAM HILL APARTMENTS in 1950, the first year after they had been built on the site of the Webb Shipbuilding Academy. Each house bears an English name, and they are grouped around a center lawn where flowers are planted. The street in the back to the left is Sedgwick Avenue. (Courtesy of The Bronx County Historical Society, New York City)

ST. NICHOLAS OF TOLENTINE CHURCH at the corner of Fordham Road and University Avenue rose out of a crowd of apartment houses and single family homes as if it were a Gothic cathedral.

(Courtesy of The Bronx County Historical Society, New York City)

THE LOEW'S GRAND THEATRE on Fordham Road and Jerome Avenue dominated the corner in 1928. To the right are the stairs leading to the Jerome Avenue-Lexington Avenue subway line. In the background to the right is the sloping roof of St. James' Episcopal Church. The apartment houses to the left helped support the shops on the corner, and this was enough to induce the owner to announce to the world that he intended to build another story on top of them.

THE LOBBY OF THE LOEW'S GRAND THEATRE on Fordham Road and Jerome Avenue in 1927 served to transport a patron into an atmosphere of a palace. A chandelier hangs from a molded ceiling over a highly polished floor. A marble staircase with carved balustrades leads to an upper level with heavy brocaded fabric on the walls.

(Courtesy of The Bronx County Historical Society, New York City)

THE STAGE OF THE LOEW'S GRAND THEATRE on Fordham Road and Jerome Avenue shows the ornate decoration of the house when it opened in 1927. The box seats, as well as the stage, had draperies and the proscenium arch had molding. There was intricate carving on the ceiling.   (Courtesy of The Bronx County Historical Society, New York City)

FORDHAM ROAD AND MORRIS AVENUE, about 1950, shows a fairly quiet scene in the morning. Here, the neighborhood bakery and the local Grant's five-and-ten-cent store border an outlet of a nationwide shoe firm, meant to appeal to shoppers coming to the Fordham Road shopping center from outside the area. Hanscom's Bakery displayed the curved lines and metal detail work which was the hallmark of the Art Deco style so prevalent in the western part of The Bronx. (Courtesy of The Bronx County Historical Society, New York City)

THE LOEW'S PARADISE THEATRE on the Grand Concourse and 188th Street was the most opulent attraction in The Bronx. Everywhere, this 4,000-seat movie palace was laced with carving, statuary, and paintings. The ceiling of the spacious theater featured twinkling stars and clouds moving over the dark blue surface. This "Showplace of The Bronx" was crowded every time it showed its first-run-in-The-Bronx feature films, but the evening's enjoyment came not only from the film but also from the surroundings which transported the patrons into a dreamland baroque palace.

(Courtesy of The Bronx County Historical Society, New York City)

THE RKO FORDHAM THEATRE is located in the heart of the shopping center at Fordham Road and Valentine Avenue, one block east of the Grand Concourse. In 1938, its marquee, emblazoned with lights, not only advertised the latest double feature but also illuminated the surrounding shops. (Courtesy of The Bronx County Historical Society, New York City)

THE GRAND CONCOURSE AND 193RD STREET in 1950 shows the increased importance of the Grand Concourse-Fordham Road shopping center. The Dollar Savings Bank is in the process of building a high office tower. Above the underpass can be seen a recruiting booth for the armed forces. The trees to the left mark Poe Park.

(Courtesy of The Bronx County Historical Society, New York City)

FORDHAM ROAD AT KINGSBRIDGE ROAD in the early 1930s shows the specialty shops on the left and the automobile traffic going over the trolley tracks embedded in the Belgian block. The small park to the right has only grass and a lone bench. The apartment house in the center rises at the corner of Valentine Avenue.

(Courtesy of The Bronx County Historical Society, New York City)

106

FORDHAM ROAD AND KINGSBRIDGE ROAD, about 1950, is congested with traffic. Shoppers line the benches in the little triangular park to the left. In the center, on the horizon, rises Keating Hall of Fordham University.

(Courtesy of The Bronx County Historical Society, New York City)

FORDHAM ROAD AND WEBSTER AVENUE in the early 1930s was full of specialty shops, but customers were not to be seen in droves. At the right is the white stone structure which served as a branch of the Corn Exchange Bank. There is very little traffic. The policeman at the left center of the picture standing in the middle of the road is directing it in the absence of traffic lights.

(Courtesy of The Bronx County Historical Society, New York City)

FORDHAM ROAD WEST OF THIRD AVENUE, 1936, shows some activity on the sidewalks of the street, with trolleys and buses passing by. Roger's Department Store is at the left and the Corn Exchange Bank is in the center.

(Courtesy of The Bronx County Historical Society, New York City)

FORDHAM ROAD EAST OF DECATUR AVENUE, about 1940, is a crowded place. Passengers waiting for their trolleys stand amid the automobile traffic, while those crossing the street scurry by. The Fordham Road station of the Third Avenue El overhead is packed with people. A park with its comfort station stands to the left. Behind it can be seen parts of the buildings of Fordham University through the trees. The cupola on the right rises above Theodore Roosevelt High School.

(Courtesy of The Bronx County Historical Society, New York City)

FORDHAM ROAD AND WEBSTER AVENUE, about 1950, proves that traffic had increased over the past decades. Buses have replaced the trolleys, and there is more automobile traffic. Roger's Department Store rises to the right. A downtown train is pulling out of the Third Avenue El station. Behind the station can be seen Theodore Roosevelt High School. The trees to the left are part of a small park. (Courtesy of The Bronx County Historical Society, New York City)

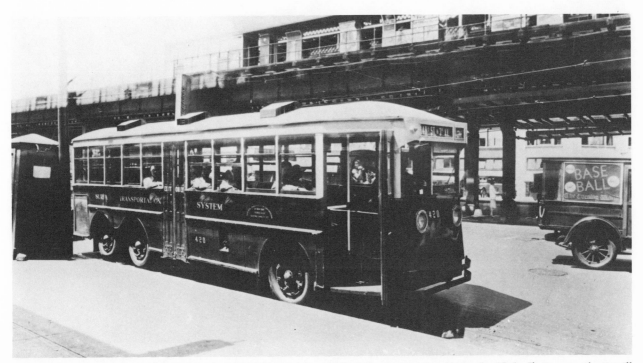

A BUS AT THIRD AVENUE AND FORDHAM ROAD, 1930, is beginning its run to the Hub. Facing north, it will make a turn to continue to its southern terminus. Behind it is the Fordham Road station of the Third Avenue El and Roger's Department Store. (Courtesy of The Bronx County Historical Society, New York City)

FORDHAM ROAD EAST OF THIRD AVENUE in the 1940s had hardly any traffic on it. The bus had started its run at City Island, while the trolleys were plying their way between Manhattan and Southern Boulevard. The trees on the left shield the buildings of Fordham University. On the right, behind the row of shops, rises Theodore Roosevelt High School.

(Courtesy of The Bronx County Historical Society, New York City)

FORDHAM UNIVERSITY in the 1930s showed a broad, green lawn with beautiful, stately trees when seen from the platform of the Third Avenue El. The auditorium building is at the left, and the building housing the administrative offices can barely be seen amid the trees behind the flagpole. A sign near the entrance directs all commercial traffic to enter at Bathgate Avenue.

(Courtesy of The Bronx County Historical Society, New York City)

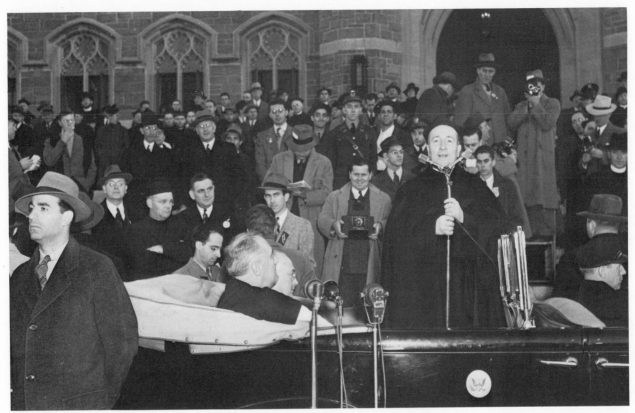

FRANKLIN D. ROOSEVELT IS WELCOMED TO FORDHAM UNIVERSITY on his campaign trip in 1940. Seated next to the President is Archbishop Francis Spellman. Standing at the microphone is Rev. Robert I. Gannon, S.J., famous Catholic orator and rector of Fordham University from 1936 to 1948.

FORDHAM ROAD AND SOUTHERN BOULEVARD, 1931, sports a comfort station to the left, the trees of the Botanical Garden behind it and the Bronx Zoo across the street.

SOUTHERN BOULEVARD SOUTH OF FORDHAM ROAD, 1920, is having its street paved. The park to the left is the Bronx Zoo. The street with the houses to the right is the end of Prospect Avenue.

FORDHAM HOSPITAL on Southern Boulevard in the 1940s. This was one of the major city hospitals in The Bronx. Taxis are arriving at the entrance to bring visitors for the patients inside.

THE BOAT HOUSE in Bronx Park at the Bronx River just north of busy West Farms Square was an oasis of tranquility. Located at the southernmost entrance to the Bronx Zoo, thousands of people flocked to the site to rent rowboats to spend some time on the cool river water contemplating the beautiful surroundings.

(Courtesy of The Bronx County Historical Society, New York City)

LAKE AGASSIZ in the Bronx Zoo was a widening of the Bronx River in the northern end of the zoo grounds. With trees in full foliage, it was a beautiful sight.

(Courtesy of the Saul Weber Collection)

THE BRONX ZOO proudly displayed a Tlinket totem pole and house on its grounds along the banks of the Bronx River in the 1920s.

(Courtesy of the Saul Weber Collection)

THE BRONX ZOO placed one terminal for its tractor-train at the West Farms entrance where the 1920s apartment houses of Bronx Park South overlooked the grounds. Crowds had to wait a long time on a summer day in the mid-1940s before they were permitted to board the vehicle.

(Courtesy of The Bronx County Historical Society, New York City)

THE BRONX ZOO in the early 1940s acquired the tractor-train, which enabled visitors to ride through the beautiful Bronx Park and see the major exhibits. However, anyone on foot had to give way to the new contraption.

THE BRONX ZOO attracted large crowds on a summer Sunday in the 1940s. The Elephant House lies beyond the trees on the left. In front of it is the ring where children could ride some animals. Those who wished to do so had to pay ten cents for the privilege at the booth to the right.

BRONX ZOO PARKING CIRCLE, 1947, is jammed with automobiles that had entered from Fordham Road, down the lane in the center of the photograph, and parked around the baroque Italian fountain. The visitors would climb the stairs on the lower left-hand corner to see the animals. (Courtesy of The Bronx County Historical Society, New York City)

THE LORILLARD MANSION in the Botanical Garden was used as a small art and science museum until it burned down in the 1920s. (Courtesy of The Bronx County Historical Society, New York City)

THE LORILLARD SNUFF MILL in the Botanical Garden was used for storage in October 1936.

THE CONSERVATORY in the Botanical Garden was a massive greenhouse with many exotic tropical plants inside.

THE PALM HOUSE INSIDE THE CONSERVATORY OF THE BOTANICAL GARDEN has the walkways covered
with overhanging palm fronds. A bench is provided beneath one of the plants for visitors to rest upon.

118

POE COTTAGE in 1926, located at the northern edge of Poe Park, has flowers planted amid two shrubs in front of the porch. A large tree at the corner provides ample shade. (Courtesy of The Bronx County Historical Society, New York City)

POE COTTAGE in 1936 has shrubs in front that nearly obscure the porch. Behind to the left can be seen an unusual eight-story 1920s apartment house on the Grand Concourse and Kingsbridge Road.

(Courtesy of The Bronx County Historical Society, New York City)

119

POE COTTAGE in March 1948 has a neatly trimmed hedge in front. Behind is a 1920s apartment house and a taxpayer with neighborhood shops on Kingsbridge Road.

POE COTTAGE was kept as neat and clean as it was when Edgar Allan Poe lived there. A visit inside would transport the onlooker to the poverty-stricken world of the famed author and poet.

FORDHAM MANOR DUTCH REFORMED CHURCH on Kingsbridge Road near Goulden Avenue in April 1934 had the look of an elegant colonial church surrounded by twentieth-century apartment houses.

BAINBRIDGE AVENUE AT 197TH STREET was a very quiet thoroughfare in 1950. Apartment houses line the sidewalks to the left, while a spacious private house and an Art Deco apartment house share the side to the right. Although there is a bus stop, cars line the curbs almost bumper to bumper.

(Courtesy of The Bronx County Historical Society, New York City)

BEDFORD PARK BOULEVARD AND DECATUR AVENUE, about 1950, is flanked by apartment houses built in the 1920s to the right and by older brownstone-type brick houses to the left. Both have shops at the sidewalk level to serve the people of the neighborhood. Above Webster Avenue in the center rises the Third Avenue El.

(Courtesy of The Bronx County Historical Society, New York City)

THE MOUNT SAINT URSULA ACADEMY rose on the side of a hill at the Bedford Park Boulevard near Marion Avenue in the 1920s.

(Courtesy of the Saul Weber Collection)

A PAGEANT AT ST. PHILIP NERI'S CHURCH SCHOOL, Grand Concourse near Bedford Park Boulevard, in the 1940s brought out the best in the schoolchildren taking part. Girls in white dresses and red sashes and boys in suits sing patriotic songs.

(Courtesy of The Bronx County Historical Society, New York City)

THE PLEDGE OF ALLEGIANCE TO THE FLAG at St. Philip Neri's Church School in the early 1940s was done with the arm toward the flag after the words "to the flag . . ." in the pledge. This was changed to keeping the hand over the heart soon after the country entered the Second World War. The girls are wearing dresses and the boys have on white shirts, ties, and knickers.   (Courtesy of The Bronx County Historical Society, New York City)

THE HUNTER COLLEGE CAMPUS during World War II served as a training station for the WAVES. Here, on October 2, 1943, Captain W. A. Amsden, former First Lady Grace Coolidge, and Bronx Borough President James J. Lyons take the salute as they review 2,500 WAVES. To the right in the rear can be seen Walton High School, an all-girl institution, and in the center beneath the canopy in the rear is the side of the huge Kingsbridge Armory.

(Courtesy of The Bronx County Historical Society, New York City)

SECURITY COUNCIL DELEGATES ARRIVE AT HUNTER COLLEGE, March 25, 1946, with a crowd gathered in front of the Gymnasium Building. The Tudor Gothic structure in the distance to the right is Gillet Hall. In the center behind the trees is the Jerome Park Reservoir. (Courtesy of The Bronx County Historical Society, New York City)

ANDREI GROMYKO MEETS BRONX BOROUGH PRESIDENT JAMES J. LYONS, 1946, when the Security Council met on the Hunter College campus. (Courtesy of The Bronx County Historical Society, New York City)

126

THE GRAND CONCOURSE AT MOSHOLU PARKWAY, 1930. The latest model city bus is beginning its run down the Grand Concourse to the Hub. To the right is the Mosholu Parkway station of the Lexington Avenue Jerome-Woodlawn subway.

(Courtesy of The Bronx County Historical Society, New York City)

KNOX PLACE JUST SOUTH OF GUN HILL ROAD in 1950 is a quiet street whose curb is used for parking. The man at the left is standing at the base of a small flight of steps leading into the courtyard of a 1920s apartment house. A small private house is tucked between two others across the street. The trees in the background are at Mosholu Parkway.

(Courtesy of The Bronx County Historical Society, New York City)

127

HULL AVENUE NORTH OF 205TH STREET suffered greatly from the record snowfall of December 26, 1947. Parked cars were buried and walking across the street was difficult.   (Courtesy of The Bronx County Historical Society, New York City)

VAN CORTLANDT AVENUE EAST AND BAINBRIDGE AVENUE was the corner on which the colonial fieldstone farmhouse known as the Valentine-Varian House stood. Newer single family homes on the left and tall apartment houses behind bordered it in April 1934.   (Courtesy of The Bronx County Historical Society, New York City)

THE RECONSTRUCTION OF THE WILLIAMSBRIDGE RESERVOIR, 1937. The old reservoir has been drained, and playground equipment and landscaping has been added to make it a new park. The curved street is Reservoir Oval, and the tunnel entrance faces Van Cortlandt Avenue East at Bainbridge Avenue.

MONTEFIORE HOSPITAL on Bainbridge Avenue and Gun Hill Road was an expanding medical facility in 1931. Across the street from the hospital itself was the nurses' residence, and the high annex to the right had been recently completed. The apartment houses across the street on the left are on Wayne Avenue.

ROCHAMBEAU AVENUE AT 206TH STREET, about 1950, shows some of the elegant apartment houses built during the 1920s. Spacious apartments inside featured three to six rooms. Amenities of living on the block included trees and shrubs, and a short one-block walk to the IND Concourse line subway, as announced on the sign affixed to the lamppost to the right. Nevertheless, many of the neighbors were beginning to own cars and there was a lack of parking space at the curb.

PERRY AVENUE AND 207TH STREET, about 1925, was occupied by a magnificent private home with a porch. Trees, shrubs, and grass are all covered by the winter's snow. (Courtesy of The Bronx County Historical Society, New York City)

KINGSBRIDGE HEIGHTS in 1949 is the forest of apartment houses occupying the hillside in the center and right of the photograph. Behind the few factory buildings in the center are the apartments on Albany Crescent and above them are those of Sedgwick Avenue. The elevated line to the left is the Broadway subway leading to the 231st Street station beyond the tree. The excavation in the foreground is for the Marble Hill Houses.

132

THE INTERIOR OF THE RKO MARBLE HILL on Broadway near 232nd Street had the ornate elements found in most motion picture palaces in 1935. Carpeted aisles muffled the feet of patrons shuffling toward their seats. Curtains not only covered the screen but also all exits. Illumination came from sconces along the walls.

(Courtesy of The Bronx County Historical Society, New York City)

RIVERDALE AVENUE AT 230TH STREET, about 1925, clearly indicates the difference between the Kingsbridge neighborhood, abounding in single family homes at the center and right of the photograph, and the Riverdale neighborhood of large estates and expansive greenery rising up the hill and to the left.

(Courtesy of The Bronx County Historical Society, New York City)

SPUYTEN DUYVIL HILL is dominated by the Henry Hudson Bridge at the right in the mid-1940s. On the horizon rises the one shaft bearing the statue of the explorer after whom the bridge is named and a new large apartment house. The hill itself is largely covered with trees and grass and dotted with small apartments and single family homes. At the base of the hill lies the Spuyten Duyvil station of the New York Central Railroad's Hudson Division. Rising from it, angling to the right, is Edsall Avenue, while Palisade Avenue skirts the rim of the cliff above.

(Courtesy of The Bronx County Historical Society, New York City)

MANHATTAN COLLEGE in the 1930s centered around its stately quadrangle. Most of the classes were held in the U-shaped structure, which is really three separate buildings connected by two huge arches. Behind the chapel bearing the white cupola is the baseball field, which doubled as a football field in the fall.

(Courtesy of The Bronx County Historical Society, New York City)

THE FREEMAN MANSION, called Wave Hill, was one of many fine estates in the Riverdale neighborhood. Fronting on Independence Avenue, it extended to the Hudson River behind it. (Courtesy of The Bronx County Historical Society, New York City)

PART OF THE FREEMAN ESTATE is in the foreground of this photograph. The view from the rear verandah of the mansion of the Freeman family in Riverdale included a panorama of the Hudson River and the Palisades in New Jersey.

BROADWAY NEAR MOSHOLU AVENUE, about 1940, has an empty appearance. The building in the center houses Paul's Restaurant, and a line of garages graces the Texaco service station next to it. The Bronx and Van Cortlandt Parks trolley is on its way to West Farms Square and has open sides for summer use.

BROADWAY AND 242ND STREET on Sunday, May 22, 1921, had crowds of people streaming to Van Cortlandt Park on the right. The line of trolleys have reached the end of their run, and the one in the foreground is in the process of starting its return trip. A crowd has gathered to board a trolley on the right track going to Yonkers.

(Courtesy of The Bronx County Historical Society, New York City)

THE VAN CORTLANDT MANSION in Van Cortlandt Park was an old colonial mansion where the caretaker would tell visitors that George Washington had visited several times. To the left of this 1937 photograph can be seen the caretaker's residence.

(Courtesy of The Bronx County Historical Society, New York City)

THE PARADE GROUND in Van Cortlandt Park, behind the mansion, was laid out for a spirited soccer game in April 1937. The hills to the left were the burial site of the old Van Cortlandt family, and anyone who climbed them could find the vault there. The poles bearing electric lines near the center mark the right of way of the Putnam Division of the New York Central Railroad.

(Courtesy of The Bronx County Historical Society, New York City)

THE DUTCH GARDENS in Van Cortlandt Park burst into glorious color as the tulips bloomed in May 1937. At the top of the formal brick staircase is the Van Cortlandt Mansion, which overlooked the formal garden. The stairs were also a place to relax and survey the peaceful scene. (Courtesy of The Bronx County Historical Society, New York City)

THE LAKE IN VAN CORTLANDT PARK is traversed by people in their rented rowboats in April 1937. At the border of the lake, to the left, are the tracks of the Putnam Division of the New York Central Railroad.

WEBSTER AVENUE NORTH OF GUN HILL ROAD, 1920, reveals a country-like setting. Electric wires are strung from poles. The high wall to the left with the iron fence above it is the eastern boundary of Woodlawn Cemetery.

WEBSTER AVENUE NORTH OF GUN HILL ROAD is being repaved by a WPA crew in 1938. A garage is on the left, small attached houses and billboards are on the right, and the trees of Woodlawn Cemetery rise to the rear.

(Courtesy of The Bronx County Historical Society, New York City)

THE THIRD AVENUE EL EXTENSION ALONG GUN HILL ROAD in 1920, under construction. The elevated line in the background services the White Plains Road line of the Lexington Avenue subway.

(Courtesy of The Bronx County Historical Society, New York City)

THE BRONX RIVER AT GUN HILL ROAD, about 1950, is enjoyed by neighborhood boys and their pet dog. The bridge above carried Gun Hill Road and the steel pillars of the Third Avenue El.

THE BRONX RIVER NORTH OF GUN HILL ROAD in 1950 reveals the Third Avenue El at the left turning into Webster Avenue near the center of the photograph. The apartment houses in the distance stand between Gun Hill Road and Woodlawn Cemetery. Commercial establishments line the west bank of the river.

(Courtesy of The Bronx County Historical Society, New York City)

143

THE BRONX RIVER SOLDIER in the Bronx River south of Gun Hill Road in 1945 was a local landmark. Everyone would wonder who he was and how he got there.   (Courtesy of The Bronx County Historical Society, New York City)

THE HAVENDER MONUMENT WORKS on Jerome Avenue near Woodlawn Cemetery around 1940 was a thriving business. The trees behind the property are in the cemetery. *(Courtesy of The Bronx County Historical Society, New York City)*

WOODLAWN CEMETERY, about 1940, was the expanse of green and tranquility it had been from the day it opened. Varieties of trees and large swaths of lawn made it a pleasant place to walk.

(Courtesy of The Bronx County Historical Society, New York City)

THE DEDICATION OF THE WESTCHESTER AVENUE BRIDGE over the Bronx River on November 1, 1938, brought out Bronx Borough President James J. Lyons (in the front row to the right) and Mayor Fiorello LaGuardia (in the front row, second from left).

(Courtesy of The Bronx County Historical Society, New York City)

THE FUELLNER FARM on Soundview and Lafayette Avenues in the 1920s was a busy place. Here, the family is gathering tomatoes to be packed in the wooden crates sitting in the field in the center to the right. The apartment houses in the background mark the course of Eastern Boulevard.

(Courtesy of the Arthur Seifert Collection)

146

AERIAL VIEW OF THE FUELLNER FARM on Soundview and Lafayette Avenues in the mid-1940s. While all the farm buildings remain, most of the top soil of this farm was removed and used in the new Parkchester development a few miles away.

(Courtesy of the Arthur Seifert Collection)

HOLY CROSS CHURCH AND SCHOOL on Soundview and Randall Avenues about 1950. In front can be seen one of the Franciscan Friars who administered the church. (Courtesy of the Arthur Seifert Collection)

GRADUATION AT THE HOLY CROSS SCHOOL at Randall and Soundview Avenues in the mid-1920s saw all the girls dressed in white, with veils and garlands. They also wore white gloves to match. (Courtesy of the Arthur Seifert Collection)

THE POOL AT THE CLASON POINT AMUSEMENT PARK at the foot of Soundview Avenue in the early 1920s had water so dark it was called "the Inkwell." Behind the fence can be seen the Ferris wheel.

(Courtesy of the Arthur Seifert Collection)

WAITING FOR THE CLASON POINT FERRY in the early 1920s. Here, the Beecher and Shaw families of Throgs Neck wait with other motorists in a line for the ferry's return from the Queens shore.

(Courtesy of The Bronx County Historical Society, New York City)

PIERS NEAR SCHURZ AVENUE IN FERRY POINT, 1948, service several rowboats.

MCDOWELL PLACE AND SCHURZ AVENUE in Ferry Point, 1948, was a desolate place. An empty lot with tall grass growing filled the corner, while frame houses formed its perimeter. Out of the picture to the right was a view of the East River.

HOUSEBOAT LIVING AT FERRY POINT, 1948, was more common than might have been supposed in the waters off the eastern shores of The Bronx. Several families lived in houseboats very much like this one.

CASTLE HILL AND LAFAYETTE AVENUES was a quiet intersection about 1925. The spire of St. Andrew's Episcopal Church dominates the scene overlooking a fenced-in green patch bearing a memorial to the dead of what was then called the World War. Traffic was so sparse that a pedestrian could easily walk his dog across the intersection without fear.

CASTLE HILL AVENUE AT 177TH STREET was a local shopping center in 1938. George Uhl's hardware store was a local landmark. To ease the rigors of the Depression and to improve the neighborhood, the WPA was building a traffic island at the intersection.

(Courtesy of The Bronx County Historical Society, New York City)

THE INTERIOR OF THE RKO CASTLE HILL at Castle Hill and Westchester Avenues reveals a simple colonial style. This 1947 photograph clearly shows that no balcony existed, and young lovers were forced to do their necking in the small orchestra.

BRUCKNER BOULEVARD AT WESTCHESTER CREEK in the mid-1940s marked the boundary of the Castle Hill neighborhood. People could dine and dance at Kaiser's near the bridge, and children attended the school on Castle Hill Avenue that can be seen beyond it. To the left can be seen the new, widened section of Bruckner Boulevard.

(Courtesy of The Bronx County Historical Society, New York City)

BRUCKNER BOULEVARD NEAR LOGAN AVENUE looking toward Tremont Avenue in the mid-1940s was an area of three- or four-story apartment houses, taxpayers, and frame dwellings. Traffic streams along Bruckner Boulevard (formerly called Eastern Boulevard). Structures at the near curb have been destroyed in preparation for the widening of the street.

(Courtesy of The Bronx County Historical Society, New York City)

BRUCKNER BOULEVARD NEAR EDISON AVENUE looking toward Logan and Hollywood Avenues in the mid-1940s was a scene of mostly frame houses. The structure at the corner of Logan Avenue is for sale with J. Clarence Davies, a Bronx-based real estate firm, as the agent. The vacant land in the foreground has been cleared to prepare for the widening of Bruckner Boulevard.   (Courtesy of The Bronx County Historical Society, New York City)

EDGEWATER PARK on Throgs Neck was a closely knit community of bungalow dwellers who rented the land on which their houses stood. This photograph, taken in 1930, clearly shows the close relationship the people there had with the water.   (Courtesy of The Bronx County Historical Society, New York City)

156

THE ICE CREAM PARLOR AT EDGEWATER PARK in the 1920s was located in a Victorian structure with gingerbread decoration. It sold delicious Horton Ice Cream.   (Courtesy of The Bronx County Historical Society, New York City)

THE CESSPOOL CLEANER AT EDGEWATER PARK in the 1920s was an example of the men who went about the streets of The Bronx selling products or services with a horse-drawn wagon.

(Courtesy of The Bronx County Historical Society, New York City)

QUADRANGLE OF FORT SCHUYLER at the tip of Throgs Neck in 1934 had a forlorn appearance. Outside the ancient walls, a lighthouse stood to guide vessels through the passage between Long Island Sound to the left and the East River to the right.

(Courtesy of The Bronx County Historical Society, New York City)

TROLLEY CAR PASSES THE NEW YORK, WESTCHESTER, AND BOSTON HEADQUARTERS on Morris Park Avenue and 180th Street in the 1930s. The building was designed in Spanish colonial style.

(Courtesy of The Bronx County Historical Society, New York City)

UNIONPORT ROAD LOOKING TOWARD TREMONT AVENUE, 1939, reveals that the old Catholic Protectory grounds have been levelled prior to the building of Parkchester. (Courtesy of The Bronx County Historical Society, New York City)

MORRIS PARK AVENUE BETWEEN MATHEWS AND BARNES AVENUES, 1922, was the site of Ed Dittmar's service station. The frame houses in the area form part of the Morris Park neighborhood.

(Courtesy of The Bronx County Historical Society, New York City)

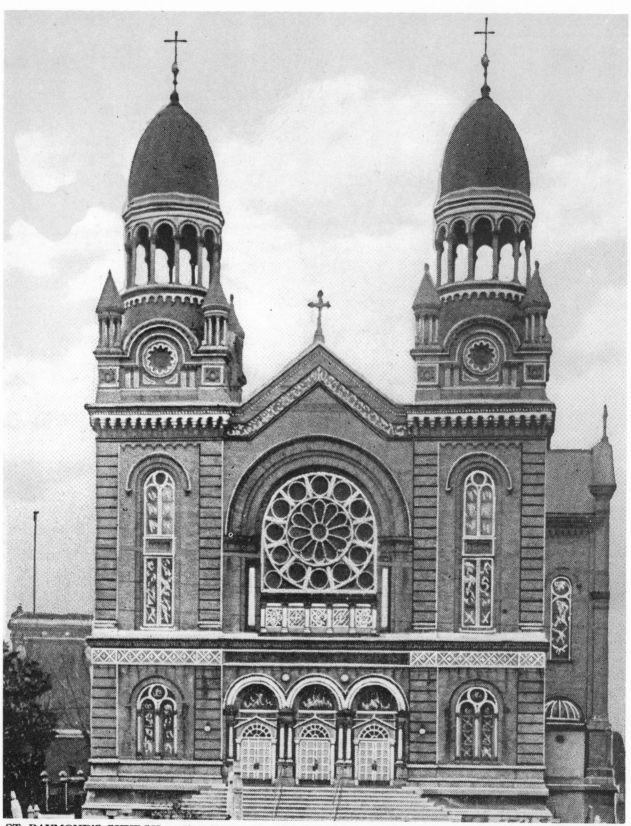

ST. RAYMOND'S CHURCH on East Tremont and Castle Hill Avenues dominated the corner with its twin cupolas. Passing a small churchyard leading to the entrance, the worshipper was swept into an interior full of light reflecting off the cream-colored walls. The number of worshippers attending Mass rose greatly when Parkchester was built nearby.

THE OLD CATHOLIC PROTECTORY GROUNDS were levelled in 1939 so that Parkchester could be built. McGraw Avenue is in the lower right-hand corner. The buildings on the horizon to the right are at Olmstead Avenue and at Purdy Street. To the left can be seen the twin cupolas of St. Raymond's Church on Tremont and Castle Hill Avenues.

THE CATHOLIC PROTECTORY at Tremont Avenue and Unionport Road in 1938 was the place where many a wayward boy would be sheltered. Baseball games were played on its grounds and the boys' band was in great demand.

METROPOLITAN OVAL, Parkchester, 1942, is a scene of tall red-brick apartment houses surrounding a pleasant park with a fountain. It is obvious that the tall trees in the park are older than the trees recently planted along the sides of the roadway. Parking space is available at the curbs.   (Courtesy of The Bronx County Historical Society, New York City)

BOROUGH PRESIDENT JAMES J. LYONS ADDRESSES A CROWD at the opening of the Parkchester Post Office in the early 1940s. The new buildings of the development rise in the background.

(Courtesy of The Bronx County Historical Society, New York City)

WESTCHESTER SQUARE AT NIGHT in the late 1930s was illuminated by electric street lamps. The elevated structure along Westchester Avenue carries the Lexington Avenue Pelham Bay local. In the center to the left is the square's park. Along the curb in the center right a horse trough still exists, despite the fact that the only vehicles in sight are cars. (Courtesy of The Bronx County Historical Society, New York City)

THE HUNTINGTON FREE LIBRARY ON WESTCHESTER SQUARE in the 1920s. Reading could be done in this charming Victorian Gothic building, but no books could be borrowed. (Courtesy of The Bronx County Historical Society, New York City)

THE CAST OF THE ST. PETER'S PARISH MUSICAL REVUE, 1948, poses for their picture. The Episcopal Church of St. Peter's on Westchester Avenue near Westchester Square had been a center of life in the community for centuries, and the musical revues carried on the tradition.   (Courtesy of The Bronx County Historical Society, New York City)

BRONX PARK EAST AND PELHAM PARKWAY, 1941, is lined with newly built Art Deco apartment houses where one and a half to five rooms are available for rental. They overlook Bronx Park to the right, and there is not much traffic on the street. Whatever there is can be serviced at the gas station on the corner.

(Courtesy of The Bronx County Historical Society, New York City)

PELHAM PARKWAY EAST OF WHITE PLAINS ROAD is a scene of bustling activity in 1928. Overlooking the broad expanse of trees on the Parkway to the left are new apartment buildings to the right. The one at the extreme right has apartments available, while the large one across the street from it is in the process of completing construction.

(Courtesy of The Bronx County Historical Society, New York City)

PELHAM PARKWAY AND EASTCHESTER ROAD was the location of the Pelham Heath Inn, a popular roadhouse when this photograph was taken in the early 1930s. (Courtesy of The Bronx County Historical Society, New York City)

THE LOEW'S POST ROAD on Boston Road and Corsa Avenue was built in 1939 near a block of twenty-eight stores to serve the Hillside Homes development. (Courtesy of The Bronx County Historical Society, New York City)

THE HILLSIDE HOUSES ARE DEDICATED on June 29, 1935, as Governor Herbert H. Lehman steps before the microphones. This apartment house complex was noted for the desirability of the basement level garden apartments.

(Courtesy of The Bronx County Historical Society, New York City)

THE ORIGINAL ORCHARD BEACH in Pelham Bay Park in the 1920s consisted of a few wooden dwellings and tents on the rocky shoreline.

(Courtesy of the Saul Weber Collection)

167

THE ORIGINAL ORCHARD BEACH in 1920 where bathers would go to a summer bungalow colony for the season.

(Courtesy of The Bronx County Historical Society, New York City)

HUNTER ISLAND INN in Pelham Bay Park was once an elegant mansion that had served as a fine restaurant for visitors enchanted with the natural surroundings and views of Long Island Sound. By October 1936, it was already abandoned and would soon be destroyed. (Courtesy of The Bronx County Historical Society, New York City)

CITY ISLAND as seen from the bridge that connects it with Pelham Bay Park in the 1920s reveals frame houses nestled among the trees. Boats of all kinds and sizes are anchored in the water. (Courtesy of the Saul Weber Collection)

THE MARSHALL MANSION in Pelham Bay Park had been a stately home and an inn near the City Island Bridge. By the time this photograph was taken in 1936, it was boarded up and would soon be demolished.

(Courtesy of The Bronx County Historical Society, New York City)

BUS ON CITY ISLAND AVENUE, 1928, making its run. The buildings along this main street in City Island are made of wood.

CITY ISLAND AVENUE near Centre Street in 1938 bears all the characteristics of a main street in New England. The Marshall Navigation School occupies its quarters in the small building to the right, while farther up the Avenue, near Schofield Street, is Burkhardt's Bar and Grill and Delicatessen. Even farther up is a candy store, a fish market, and other shops serving the people of the island.

233RD STREET AND KATONAH AVENUE was a fairly deserted corner about 1930. In one frame house, an automobile owner could buy tires and gas and step into Whelpley's Ice Cream Parlor for a treat. At that time, Katonah Avenue was still a dirt road.

233RD STREET AND WEBSTER AVENUE shows a cluster of cars in 1938. Traffic is forced to exit from the Bronx River Parkway southbound to the left, cross the railway tracks flanked by Woodlawn Station on 233rd Street, and re-enter the parkway to the right. Across Bronx Boulevard from Woodlawn Station is Mayer's Restaurant. On the horizon of 233rd Street is the elevated station of the IRT White Plains Road line.

THE BRONX RIVER BENEATH THE 233RD STREET BRIDGE in December 1947 makes the record snowfall of that month look benign in this picturesque scene.   (Courtesy of The Bronx County Historical Society, New York City)

THE 238TH STREET BRIDGE over the Bronx River, undergoing repairs, about 1950. At its eastern end is a small manufacturing center. Beyond the factories are some frame houses with trees on the sidewalk. In the distance in the center is the 238th Street station of the White Plains Road line.   (Courtesy of The Bronx County Historical Society, New York City)

WHITE PLAINS ROAD AT 241ST STREET, 1947, is the point where the trolleys meet the end of the White Plains Road elevated subway line. Shops in the vicinity thrive on the trade that the trolleys bring.

(Courtesy of The Bronx County Historical Society, New York City)

SETON FALLS PARK in the winter of 1941 was a wonderful sight with its rolling slopes and soaring trees. The benches were located at the picnic ground there.

(Courtesy of The Bronx County Historical Society, New York City)

233RD STREET AND PROVOST AVENUE in July 1941 is dominated by Scharff's service station.

DYRE AVENUE NEAR BOSTON ROAD, about 1930, is a stop for the short trolley which ran over the Dyre Avenue route. When going very fast, it seemed to pitch forward and backward as if at sea.

BOSTON ROAD OPPOSITE THE FOOT OF DYRE AVENUE was the location of Breinlinger's Bar and Grill in the 1940s, a noted neighborhood watering hole.

REAR OF HOUSES ON PROVOST AVENUE NEAR LIGHT STREET, 1940, faces an empty lot. Each of the frame houses is slightly different but all are about the same height. Not all have garages in the back. Some have wooden poles erected from which a clothesline is hung to the house, and some have wet wash hanging out to dry.

BOSTON ROAD AT BAYCHESTER AVENUE, about 1950, still had many wide-open spaces and empty lots. The scene looked very much like the outskirts of a small town.　　　(Courtesy of The Bronx County Historical Society, New York City)

EDSON AVENUE JUST NORTH OF ADEE AVENUE, 1940, is a scene of open spaces, empty lots, and occasional frame houses.　　　(Courtesy of The Bronx County Historical Society, New York City)

MARSHLAND EAST OF BAYCHESTER AVENUE looking toward the Hutchinson River, 1950, reveals a flat landscape. Across the river lies Pelham Bay Park. The bridge services the Hutchinson River Parkway. The two towers to the right mark the New Haven Railroad's tracks. The rectangular stone object sticking up out of the marsh in the foreground is the remains of an old mill. (Courtesy of The Bronx County Historical Society, New York City)

TWO SYMBOLS OF THE BRONX, Borough President James J. Lyons and Gertrude Berg, who played Molly Goldberg on radio. Together in the Borough President's office in the Bronx County Building, they boost the Greater New York Fund.

About The Bronx County Historical Society

The Bronx County Historical Society was founded in 1955 for the purpose of collecting and preserving manuscripts, books, and historical objects connected with the history, heritage, and growth of The Bronx, and to promote knowledge, interest, and research in these fields. The Society operates the Museum of Bronx History, Edgar Allan Poe Cottage, a research library, and the County Archives; conducts historical walking tours and educational programs; sponsors various expeditions to recover artifacts of past Bronxites; erects plaques at historical sites; and produces the "OUT OF THE PAST" radio show. The Society is active in furthering the arts, preserving the natural resources of The Bronx, and creating a sense of pride in the Bronx Community. **For further information, write to The Bronx County Historical Society, 3266 Bainbridge Avenue, Bronx, New York 10467.**

Index